DI[AL] M
FOR MURDER

A COLLAGE FOR VOICES
BY FREDERICK KNOTT

★

★

DRAMATISTS
PLAY SERVICE
INC.

DIAL "M" FOR MURDER
Copyright © Renewed 1980, 1981, 1982, Frederick Knott
Copyright © 1953, 1954, Frederick Knott
Copyright © 1952, Frederick Knott
as an unpublished dramatic composition

All Rights Reserved

SPECIAL NOTE

DIAL "M" FOR MURDER was first presented on the stage by James P. Sherwood at the Westminster Theatre, London, on June 19, 1952. It was directed by John Fernald and the setting was by Paul Mayo. The cast was as follows:

SHEILA WENDICE .... Jane Baxter
MAX HALLIDAY .... Alan MacNaughtan
TONY WENDICE .... Emrys Jones
CAPTAIN LESGATE .... Olaf Pooley
INSPECTOR HUBBARD .... Andrew Cruickshank

DIAL "M" FOR MURDER was first presented in America by James P. Sherwood at the Plymouth Theatre, New York City, on October 29, 1952. It was staged by Reginald Denham and the setting and lighting were by Peter Larkin. The cast was as follows:

MARGOT WENDICE .... Gusti Huber
MAX HALLIDAY .... Richard Derr
TONY WENDICE .... Maurice Evans
CAPTAIN LESGATE .... Anthony Dawson
INSPECTOR HUBBARD .... John Williams
THOMPSON .... Porter Van Zandt

SYNOPSIS OF SCENES

The action of the play takes place in the living room of the Wendices' apartment in London.

ACT I

Scene 1—A Friday evening in September.
Scene 2—An hour later.

ACT II

Scene 1—Saturday evening.
Scene 2—Later that night.
Scene 3—Sunday morning.

ACT III

A few months later. Early afternoon.

PRODUCTION NOTE

The scissors stabbing in Act II, Scene 2 can be done in either of two ways: Margot can pretend to stab Lesgate with the scissors and he will fall in such a way that the audience can imagine the scissors are in his back, without actually seeing them. Or, a device can be arranged whereby a pair of "trick" scissors come out of Lesgate's back with a spring device controlled by Lesgate himself.

In any event, Margot, after "stabbing" Lesgate, should place the scissors in the drawer of the desk, which is left slightly open. This drawer should have a felt pad so that the scissors dropping in will make no noise.

NOTE: If Margot should drop the scissors on the floor during the struggle, it will be just too bad! For this reason, it is a good idea to have the scissors secured to the table with Scotch tape so that they do not get knocked off in the struggle.

DIAL "M" FOR MURDER

ACT I

SCENE 1

The living room of the Wendices' flat in London.

It is about 6:20 P. M. on a Friday in September.

This is the ground-floor apartment of a large house which has been converted into apartments. At R. are French windows which look out on to Charrington Gardens. There is a small terrace immediately outside. The heavy full-length curtains are at present drawn open. Inside the windows are shutters. These are folded back into the wall and are hardly noticeable. The fireplace is D. L. A clock is on the mantel. U. L. is a door leading to the bedroom, at the back there is a small hall. R. of the hall is the entrance to the kitchen. Back center of the hall is the entrance door to the apartment (hall door).

As the curtain rises this door is closed. It has a Yale-type lock. When this door is open we can see through into a narrow passage outside which leads L. to the street door. Back of the passage is a staircase leading up (from L. to R.) to the apartment above. The stairs pass the hall doorway at about the fifth step. Inside the hall door and to the L. is a coat rack. R. of the hall door, against the back wall of the hall, is a chair. At the back on the extreme R. there are shelves with books in the top and bottles and drinking glasses on the bottom shelf. In the wall on the extreme L. there are corresponding shelves. Inside this are Tony's silver tennis trophies, a tennis racket is on the top shelf and on each side of the shelves, on the walls, are tennis photographs. In the extreme R. upstage corner is a standard lamp (floor lamp). R. C. is a flat table-desk on which there are a telephone and address book and a desk diary. (The

5

telephone is on the upstage end of desk.) The desk chair has its back to the windows. Below the desk is a wastepaper basket. L. C. is a sofa. R. of this is a stool. Behind sofa is an oblong table on which there is a silver cigarette case, an ash tray, and a vase of flowers. D. L. is a chair and behind this chair is a small wall table with a wicker mending basket filled with stockings, scissors, etc. Below the sofa is a low, round coffee table. There is a chandelier (or overhead lights) over the C. of the room, and two wall brackets in the L. wall above the fireplace. Both of these are controlled by light switches inside and at R. of the hall door. The standard lamp is switched on and off at the standard lamp itself. At present no lights are on, it still being daylight outside, but the light begins to fade during the first scene between Max and Margot. The fire is burning brightly and the hall door is closed. As the curtain rises, Margot is handing Max a drink. They are both seated on the sofa. She suddenly hears something in the passage outside, rises and goes to the hall door, which she opens and peeps through for a moment. Then she closes the hall door and turns to Max.

MARGOT. (*A little worried.*) For a moment I thought it was Tony. I'm sorry I interrupted you. What were we talking about . . .?

MAX. I was just telling you that I murdered exactly fifty-two people since I saw you last.

MARGOT. (*With a laugh, picks up her drink from coffee table. Sits on sofa.*) Oh, yes—one a week. How did you do it?

MAX. Every way I could think of. I electrocuted some in their baths, locked others in the garage with the motor running or pushed them through windows and over cliffs. Other weeks I preferred to poison, shoot, strangle, stab, slug or suffocate.

MARGOT. Just according to how you felt?

MAX. When you write for that kind of television you don't have time to feel anything.

MARGOT. Where do you get all your ideas from?

MAX. Oh—newspaper stories—police files—bad dreams—other writers . . .

MARGOT. You once told me you'd never write anything that wasn't original.

6

MAX. Huh—you try being original fifty-two times a year!

MARGOT. Suppose you just dry up and can't think of anything?

MAX. If it comes to that I just use my three hats.

MARGOT. What do you mean?

MAX. I've got three old hats marked: Who kills who, How, and Why.

MARGOT. Which is what? I mean what's Why?

MAX. Why is the motive for killing. You've got to have a motive, you know. There are only five important ones. Fear—jealousy—money—revenge—and protecting someone you love. I just write them down on pieces of paper and pick one out of the Why hat.

MARGOT. Sounds rather like sorting the week's washing.

MAX. It's about as artistic as that. But better paid. It's no more frustrating than writing plays that aren't produced or novels that aren't published. . . . And don't forget this: It all goes to prove that WITO makes teeth bright—white and *bite!*

MARGOT. (*Laughs.*) Let's have your glass, Max.

MAX. No . . . I'm all right, thanks.

MARGOT. I could hardly believe it when I heard your voice. At first I thought you were phoning from New York.

MAX. Yes, I thought you were shouting a little louder than necessary. As a matter of fact I was just around the corner. (*A pause auxiously.*) Was it all right . . . my phoning like that?

MARGOT. Yes, of course.

MAX. Was that—Tony who answered?

MARGOT. Yes, it was. (*An awkward pause.*) I do hope he isn't going to be too late. Poor darling. He always gets caught when we're going to the theater. (*Pause.*) So you're not here on a holiday—this time?

MAX. No, not this time. I came over to write some short TV films. After that I think I'll knock off for a year and write that novel. I've got to write it some day.

MARGOT. Another crime story?

MAX. I have to stick to crime—it's my stock in trade. But there's no reason why a murder story can't be as good as anything else. And I think I could write a good one if I took the time. I thought of a pretty fair gimmick on the plane coming over. There's a pair of twins—identical—one lives in Paris and the other in New York —all of a sudden they both decide to . . . (*Margot has been growing anxious and loses interest in all this.*)

MARGOT. (*Interrupting.*) Max, before Tony comes I ought to explain something.

MAX. Yes?

MARGOT. I didn't tell him anything about us.

MAX. Oh.

MARGOT. When you rang up yesterday, I just said that you were a television writer I'd met when he was in America.

MAX. Well, that's true enough.

MARGOT. I said I'd met you again just before you went back to New York and you promised to look us up if you ever came back.

MAX. I see.

MARGOT. Max, I know you think it's silly, but when you get to know Tony, you'll understand why.

MAX. Margot, I'd like to get one thing straight. (*Rises and sits on arm of sofa.*) Things are O.K. now between you and Tony?

MARGOT. They couldn't be better. And I want to keep them that way.

MAX. I'm very glad—at least I guess I will be when I get used to the idea.

MARGOT. There's something else, Max.

MAX. Yes?

MARGOT. I wasn't going to tell you but . . .

MAX. Come on, let's have it . . .

MARGOT. Well, you remember those letters you wrote me?

MAX. Of course.

MARGOT. After I read them I burnt them. I thought it best. All except one. You probably know the one I mean.

MAX. I can guess. I never should have written it.

MARGOT. I know. But I loved it just the same. I used to carry it round wherever I went. Then one day Tony and I were going to spend the week end with some friends in the country. While we were waiting on the platform I noticed my handbag was missing . . . and the letter was inside.

MAX. I see. . . . Where was this?

MARGOT. Victoria Station. I thought I must have left it in the restaurant but when I went to look for it, it had gone.

MAX. You never found it?

MARGOT. I recovered the handbag about two weeks later from the lost and found. But the letter wasn't there. (*Pause.*) Then a week after I received a note. It told me what I had to do to get the letter back.

MAX. Go on.

MARGOT. I was to draw fifty pounds from my bank in five-pound notes, then change them for used one-pound notes. It said that if I went to the police or told anyone else—he would show the letter to my husband.

MAX. May I see it? (*Margot exits into bedroom. Max gets up and paces uneasily around the room. He takes a cigarette from the silver box on table behind sofa and lights it. Then Margot enters from bedroom holding two white envelopes. She hands one of these to Max who takes out the note and examines it.*) Printed—all capitals. Anyone could have done this. (*Margot hands him the other envelope.*)

MARGOT. Then—two days later—I got this one. (*Max takes out the second note.*)

MAX. (*Glancing at the postmarks.*) Both mailed in Brixton. (*Reading.*) "Tie up money in a package and mail to John S. King, 23 Newport Street, Brixton, S.W.9. You will get your letter by return." Well, of all the . . .

MARGOT. That's a little shop. People use it as a forwarding address.

MAX. Did you mail the money?

MARGOT. Yes, but the letter was never returned. . . . So after waiting two weeks I went there. They said they'd never heard of a man by that name, and the parcel was still there. It had never been opened.

MAX. Well, I suppose that's something. (*Max puts the notes back in the envelopes and puts them into his wallet.*) May I keep these?

MARGOT. (*Hesitates.*) Yes. . . . If you like.

MAX. You didn't tell Tony?

MARGOT. No, I didn't tell anyone. (*Pause.*) I can't understand why the man didn't collect the money.

MAX. He was probably in jail by that time. (*Pause.*) You never heard from him again?

MARGOT. No.

MAX. Well, let me know if you do. I'll find him and fix him so he can't read, let alone write. (*Pause.*) Is that why you asked me to stop writing?

MARGOT. Yes. I was in an awful panic. I imagined that every letter you wrote me would be opened and read by someone.

MAX. Why didn't you tell me?

MARGOT. You couldn't have done anything. You would probably have made me tell Tony and the police. As it was only fifty pounds I thought I'd pay up and have done with it.

MAX. Margot, are you ever going to tell Tony—about us?

MARGOT. (*Horrified.*) No. I couldn't possibly tell him. Not now.

MAX. Why not? Don't you think we'd all get on better in the end if . . .

MARGOT. Please, Max, I know Tony—you don't.

MAX. You don't have to tell me. Just the thought of meeting him makes me, shall we say, uncomfortable.

MARGOT. Oh, you'll get on fine. He's changed a lot this last year. . . . Now, he's a model husband. (*Slowly and thoughtfully.*) In fact, it was exactly a year ago that it happened.

MAX. What happened?

MARGOT. Tony suddenly grew up. He seemed to change overnight from a rather selfish little person into a perfectly reasonable grownup. You remember that night—I came to say good-bye?

MAX. How could I forget? Tony had gone off to play in a tennis tournament.

MARGOT. He did—but he came back. I'm not much good at writing about things like this, so I didn't try. But when I left you that night I came back here. I sat down on the sofa and had a good cry. Then I fell asleep. When I woke up he was standing in the hall with all his bags and tennis rackets. He just said that he had decided to give up tennis for good and settle down.

MAX. Just like that? (*Margot gets up. Takes Max's glass and hers to drink shelf in* R. *bookcase and pours out drinks.*)

MARGOT. Just like that. Of course I didn't believe him at first. I'd got so used to tagging around after him wherever he went, I could see no end to it. But he meant it all right. He went out the very *next* day and got himself a job. (*A church clock chimes.*) What were we doing—exactly a year ago?

MAX. I was putting the mushrooms into the spaghetti. I nearly turned round and said, "I can't go through with this. Let's find Tony and have it out with him."

MARGOT. I felt that way, too. I wanted so much to say something—and all I could do was to stand there—quite uselessly—with a drip on the end of my nose. What did you do when I'd gone?

MAX. I walked along the Embankment and stared at the Chelsea gas works.

MARGOT. (*With a laugh, crossing to Max.*) Were you thinking about the gas works—or me?

MAX. Neither. I was writing a story. I always do when I'm miserable.

MARGOT. A sad story?

MAX. A triumphant story—my hero was an eminent writer coming from America with his pockets full of money ready to snatch his lady love from the arms of her jealous husband.

MARGOT. (*Smiling.*) Only to find that husband and wife were very happy, thank you.

MAX. And that he was very glad to know it.

MARGOT. (*Handing Max his glass.*) Max, let's drink to—the way things turn out.

MAX. (*Raising glass to Margot.*) Way things turn . . . (*But before they can drink, there is the sound of a key in the hall door. They both turn toward it, as if it had interrupted their toast. Tony enters. He is thirty-four and has an easy charm. His mind is always active and he usually seems very sure of himself.*)

MARGOT. Oh, there you are. . . . We thought you were never coming. . . . What have you been up to?

TONY. Sorry, darling. The boss blew in just as I was leaving. (*As Tony takes off his overcoat and hangs it up on coat rack, Max stands a little awkwardly, facing hall.*)

MARGOT. Tony, this is Max Halliday.

TONY. Hullo, Max.

MAX. (*Shaking hands.*) Tony . . .

TONY. I'm terribly sorry to be so late. Has Margot been looking after you all right? How's your drink? (*Tony crosses to drink shelf and mixes himself drink. Margot sits on sofa.*)

MARGOT. We've been drinking ourselves silly waiting for you.

TONY. Well, how do you like it over here, Max?

MAX. Fine.

TONY. Is this your first visit to London?

MAX. Uh—no—I was here a year ago for a vacation.

TONY. Oh, yes, that's right. Margot told me. You write for the radio, don't you?

11

MAX. Television—for my sins.

TONY. Ah, yes. Television, poor fellow. Are you staying long?

MAX. I'm not sure. I've some writing to do. When that's finished I'd like to stay a while longer and do some traveling.

TONY. That's a good idea. But don't spend all your time in museums and cathedrals. Once you've seen one, you've seen the lot, if you ask me. Do you fish?

MAX. No, I'm afraid I don't.

TONY. Pity. If you did I'd suggest you went up to Scotland for the . . .

MARGOT. He doesn't fish, darling.

TONY. No, he doesn't. I guess that's that. Well, if you want showing around any time just let us know. (*To Margot.*) Darling, we could take Max to the Tower of London.

MAX. I'm afraid I've already been there.

TONY. Oh, what a shame! I've always wanted to go to the Tower. But seriously, Max, if there's anything we can do any time . . .

MAX. Thank you, Tony. I'll remember that.

MARGOT. Darling, it's getting late. Did you reserve the table?

TONY. Yes. Seven o'clock.

MARGOT. (*Rising.*) Well, come on then. (*Moving toward bedroom.*) Get your coats on.

TONY. Oh, darling. Slight alteration in plans.

MARGOT. (*Turning.*) Now don't say you can't go.

TONY. I'm afraid so. Old man Burgess is flying to Brussels on Sunday and we all have to get our monthly reports in by tomorrow.

MARGOT. Oh, no! Can't you do it when you get back tonight?

TONY. 'Fraid not. It will take hours. I shall have to fake half of it.

MARGOT. Can you join us after the theater? We might go somewhere.

TONY. Give me a ring in the intermission. If I'm inspired I might make it . . .

MARGOT. Do try. I'll just get my things, Max. (*Margot exits to bedroom.*)

TONY. (*Crosses to Max and hands him theater tickets.*) Here are the tickets, Max.

MAX. Thanks.

TONY. I'm afraid this is extremely rude of me.

MAX. Not at all. I'm sorry you can't come, though.

TONY. You must come to dinner one night.

MAX. Thanks, I'd like to.

TONY. I say—are you doing anything tomorrow night?

MAX. Saturday. I don't think so.

TONY. (*Delighted.*) That's perfect. How would you like to come to a stag party—just down the road?

MAX. (*Puzzled.*) A stag party?

TONY. Yes. Some American boys have been playing tennis all over the Continent and we're giving them a sort of farewell dinner.

MAX. But I'm no tennis player.

TONY. That doesn't matter. You know New York and all that. (*Margot enters from bedroom. She wears overcoat and carries handbag.*) Darling. Max is coming to the party tomorrow night.

MARGOT. Oh, good. (*To Max.*) You'd better drop in here first and have a drink.

TONY. That's the idea.

MARGOT. (*To Tony.*) By the way, aren't you dressing?

TONY. Dinner jackets—yes. (*To Max.*) Is that all right?

MAX. Well, no. My trunk was supposed to arrive today, but—er—it hasn't.

TONY. (*Worried.*) Oh. (*Pause.*) You could rent one, of course.

MARGOT. Don't be silly. Darling, it isn't that important.

TONY. Just a minute. I've got an idea. (*Tony exits quickly into bedroom, leaving door open.*)

MARGOT. Now we really are going to be late.

MAX. Shall I try and get a taxi?

MARGOT. No. We can usually pick one up. (*Glancing at bedroom.*) Tony, we must go. (*Enter Tony with dinner jacket.*)

TONY. Hold it a second. Just try this on, Max.

MARGOT. What on earth?

TONY. It's only my old single-breasted but it might do. (*As Max takes off coat reluctantly.*)

MAX. Look—if dressing is as important as all this—let's forget it, shall we?

TONY. Nonsense. (*Tony helps Max on with dinner jacket.*)

MARGOT. That dreadful old thing—it reeks of moth balls.

MAX. Well, they say that writers will do anything for a square meal.

TONY. Oh. it does look a little meager, doesn't it? (*Max gestures, indicating that dinner jacket is too small. Margot helps Max off with dinner jacket and Tony helps him on with coat.*)

MARGOT. I refuse to let you send Max out looking like a scarecrow. Surely he can go as he is. (*Throws dinner jacket to Tony.*)

MAX. Anyway, my stuff ought to be here by tomorrow. Let's hope that it is.

MARGOT. Come on, Max, let's go before he tries on the pants! (*Margot and Max exit through hall door and out* L. *Tony stands in open doorway and watches them go.*)

TONY. Enjoy yourselves. Hey, Max!

MAX. (*Offstage* L.) Yes?

TONY. Try and sell the odd ticket and have a drink on the proceeds. Good-bye—have a good time. (*Tony closes the door. Turns bracket lights off and crosses to curtains. He closes curtains, switches on standard lamp and turns to telephone. After staring at the phone for a few seconds he picks it up and dials. After a pause Lesgate's voice can be heard in the phone receiver.*)

LESGATE. Hullo.

TONY. Hullo? Hampstead 2837?

LESGATE. Yes.

TONY. Could I speak to Captain Lesgate, please?

LESGATE. Speaking.

TONY. Oh, good evening. You don't know me; my name's Fisher. . . . I understand you have a car for sale.

LESGATE. An American car.

TONY. That's right; I saw it at your garage. How much are you asking?

LESGATE. Eleven hundred.

TONY. Eleven hundred! I see. It certainly looks just the job for me but I don't like the price much.

LESGATE. I didn't like it when I bought it.

TONY. (*With a laugh.*) Now when can we meet?

LESGATE. How about tomorrow afternoon?

TONY. I don't think I can manage that. (*Pause.*) No, I can't. And I'm going to Liverpool on Sunday. I was rather hoping . . . I say, I suppose you couldn't come round to my home tonight?

LESGATE. Where is it?

TONY. Maida Vale—I'd call on you only—I've twisted my knee rather badly.

LESGATE. Oh, I'm sorry. What's your address?

TONY. 61a Charrington Gardens.

LESGATE. Harrington . . .

TONY. No—Charrington.

LESGATE. Charrington . . .

TONY. That's right. Turn left at the underground. It's about two minutes' walk.

LESGATE. I'll be there in about an hour.

TONY. About an hour? That's extremely good of you. (*Anxiously.*) By the way, will you be bringing the car?

LESGATE. I'm afraid I can't tonight because it's . . .

TONY. (*Relieved.*) That doesn't matter. I had a good look at it. Perhaps you would bring the registration book and any necessary papers.

LESGATE. Of course.

TONY. I don't see why we shouldn't settle the whole thing here and now—provided you drop the price sufficiently.

LESGATE. I'm afraid that's quite out of the question.

TONY. Huh! We'll see what a couple of drinks can do.

LESGATE. (*Amused.*) Huh, huh, huh.

TONY. Huh, huh, huh. Well—good-bye.

LESGATE. Good-bye. (*Hangs up.*)

TONY. (*Hangs up.*) Captain Lesgate!

CURTAIN

ACT I

SCENE 2

The same. One hour later. The room is softly lit by the standard lamp and wall brackets. A pair of white cotton gloves lies on the stool.

As the curtain rises, Tony enters from the bedroom carrying an old leather suitcase which he places carefully against the wall L. of R. bookcase. Then he turns and surveys the room. He looks at the cotton gloves for a moment, then goes and picks them up and lays them neatly on the L. arm of the sofa. He considers the effect and is satisfied. He then starts for the bedroom. The doorbell rings and interrupts him. He turns and deliberately assumes a painful limp. He opens the hall door. Lesgate stands outside wearing an overcoat.

15

LESGATE. Mr. Fisher?

TONY. Yes. Captain Lesgate?

LESGATE. Yes.

TONY. Do come in. This is very good of you. Let me have your coat. (*He takes it and hangs it up on coat rack.*) Have any difficulty finding your way?

LESGATE. None at all. (*They enter the room.*)

TONY. Do sit down.

LESGATE. Thank you. (*Lesgate remains standing.*)

TONY. Now, how about a drink? (*Tony limps to the drink shelf. Lesgate watches him curiously for a few moments.*)

LESGATE. I can't help thinking I've seen you before somewhere.

TONY. (*Looking up sharply.*) Funny you should say that. The moment I opened the door I . . . (*He stops suddenly.*) Wait a minute . . . Lesgate? You're not Lesgate—Swann! C. J. Swann —or was it C. A.?

LESGATE. C. A. . . . you've a better memory than I have . . . Fisher? When did we meet?

TONY. Weren't you at Cambridge?

LESGATE. Yes.

TONY. Must be twenty years ago. You wouldn't remember me. . . . I only came your last year.

LESGATE. Well! What a coincidence! (*They shake hands.*)

TONY. (*Going to drink shelf.*) This calls for a special drink. I was planning to palm you off with an indifferent port. Let's see what we have here. (*Holding up the brandy.*) How about this?

LESGATE. Perfect. (*Sits on sofa.*) By the way—how did you know my car was for sale? (*Tony pours brandy into two glasses before answering. Puts brandy bottle on desk.*)

TONY. Your garage told me.

LESGATE. That's odd. I don't think I mentioned it to anyone there.

TONY. I was stopping for a fill-up. I told them I was looking for an American car and they gave me your phone number. I say, it is for sale, isn't it?

LESGATE. (*Laughing.*) Well, of course.

TONY. (*Limps painfully to Lesgate.*) Good. But I refuse to discuss the price until you've had at least three brandies. (*Tony hands Lesgate his glass.*)

LESGATE. (*Taking it.*) I warn you. I drive a hard bargain, drunk or sober.

TONY. So do I. (*They laugh.*)

LESGATE. You know, I think I must have seen you since we left Cambridge.

TONY. Ever been to Wimbledon?

LESGATE. That's it—Wendice—Tony Wendice . . . (*Bewildered.*) Then what's all this about Fisher?

TONY. (*With a teasing glance.*) What's all this about Lesgate? (*Lesgate looks embarrassed.*) Do you like a cigar?

LESGATE. (*Taking out pipe.*) I'll stick to this pipe, if you don't mind. (*Tony hesitates for a split second as if this throws him a little, then, turning away.*)

TONY. That's one habit you've changed.

LESGATE. Oh. (*Tony goes to* L. *wall and takes down a framed photograph of a group of young men at dinner.*)

TONY. I remember at college you always used to smoke rather expensive cigars. Wait a minute, I think I have a picture of you. (*Showing the photograph to Lesgate.*) Yes, look, here's an old photo of you at a reunion dinner. . . . There you are on the right with the biggest cigar in the business.

LESGATE. (*Amused.*) Huh! That was the first and last reunion I ever went to. What a murderous thug I look.

TONY. (*Even more amused.*) Yes—you do rather. Of course, I always remember you because of the College Ball. (*Pause.*) You were the treasurer, weren't you?

LESGATE. Honorary treasurer. I used to organize the beastly things.

TONY. Yes. Some of the ticket money was stolen, wasn't it? (*Tony sits on sofa.*)

LESGATE. That's right. Nearly a hundred pounds. I'd left it in a cash box in my study. In the morning, it had gone. Still makes me sweat to think of it.

TONY. It was the college porter, of course.

LESGATE. Yes, poor old Alfred. He never could back a winner. They found the cash box in his back garden. . . .

TONY. . . . but not the money. (*Lesgate hands the picture back to Tony who puts it on coffee table.*)

LESGATE. Good lord, twenty years ago!

TONY. What are you doing nowadays? (*Pause.*)

LESGATE. I deal in property. (*Changing the subject.*) I don't follow tennis very closely. Did you play at Wimbledon this year?

TONY. No. I've given up tennis or rather tennis gave me up. One has to earn a living some time, and I'd had a pretty good run for my money. I went round the world three times.

LESGATE. I suppose you were treated like a film star?

TONY. Film stars get paid.

LESGATE. There is that.

TONY. Of course I managed to save a bit on expenses. In seven years I put away just over a thousand pounds. Not much compared with your film stars!

LESGATE. What are you doing now? Making up for lost time?

TONY. I sell sports equipment. Not very lucrative but it gives me plenty of spare time.

LESGATE. (*Looking round the room.*) Well, I'm here to tell you you manage to run a very comfortable place.

TONY. (*Modestly.*) My wife has some money of her own. Otherwise I should hardly feel like blowing a thousand pounds on your car.

LESGATE. Eleven hundred. Yes, people with capital don't realize how lucky they are. I'm already resigned to living on what I can earn. (*Pause.*)

TONY. (*Thoughtfully.*) Of course, you can still marry for money. (*Pause.*)

LESGATE. Yes, I suppose some people make a business of that.

TONY. (*Quietly.*) I know I did. (*Pause.*)

LESGATE. (*With a laugh.*) You mean the girl you fell in love with happened to have some money of her own.

TONY. No. (*Pause.*) I always intended to marry for money. I had to. Whilst I was in first-class tennis I met wealthy people all over the world—I was somebody—while my wind lasted! I decided to snap up the first chance I got. I nearly married a tubby Boston deb with five million dollars; it got as far as pictures in the papers and then she threw me over for an heir to a chain of grocery stores. Funny how they stick together. I finally settled for a good deal less—a lot more easily. My wife had been a fan of mine for some time. (*Pause.*)

LESGATE. Well—that's putting it pretty bluntly.

TONY. Have I shocked you?

LESGATE. No, I always admire a man who knows what he wants.

18

TONY. To know what you want *to pay for*—that's the thing. Everything has its price. People fail because they want to buy cheap. I've learnt to pay a big price for anything I really want. . . . I usually get it.

LESGATE. Yes, I'm sure you do. (*Looking at his wrist watch.*) I haven't a great deal of time . . .

TONY. I was telling you about my wife. She got her money from her late aunt, who got it from her late husband; who got it from his first wife. Of course, a large chunk gets lopped off every time somebody dies but quite a bit has managed to filter through.

LESGATE. (*Joking.*) You say you married for money. Why do you think she married you?

TONY. (*Quite simply.*) I was a tennis star. She would never have married a commercial salesman.

LESGATE. But you've given up tennis. She hasn't left you. (*Pause.*)

TONY. She nearly did. (*Tony starts to get up rather painfully.*)

LESGATE. (*Rising.*) Let me; Wendice, you've got a groggy knee.

TONY. Oh, thanks, old boy. Let's have that bottle over here, shall we?

LESGATE. Good idea. (*Lesgate collects brandy from desk; he pours brandy into Tony's glass and then into his own. Tony watches him all the time.*)

TONY. Would you like to hear about it?

LESGATE. Hear what?

TONY. About my wife—how she nearly left me.

LESGATE. It's your privilege—you're the host.

TONY. To be frank, I think you might help. Just man to man advice, you know.

LESGATE. I'm at your service. (*Lesgate puts bottle down on coffee table and sits down.*)

TONY. After we were married I played in the various championships and Margot tagged along. I think she found it all a bit much. Hospitality—outside this country—can be pretty exhausting. When we got back she tried to persuade me to give up tennis and play husband instead. (*Rises.*) In the end, we compromised. I went alone to America for the grass court season and returned after the National Championships. I soon realized that a lot had happened while I was away. For one thing—she wasn't in love with me any more. There were phone calls that would end abruptly if I hap-

19

pened to walk in. And there was an old school friend she used to visit from time to time. Then one day we had a row; I wanted to play in a covered court tournament and as usual she didn't want me to go. I was in the bedroom—the phone rang. It all sounded pretty urgent. After that she seemed rather keen that I should play in that tournament after all, so I packed my kit into the car and drove off. (*Pause.*) I parked the car two streets away and walked back on my tracks. Ten minutes later she came out of this house and took a taxi. I took another. (*Pause.*) Her old school friend lived in a studio in Chelsea. I could see them through the studio window as he cooked spaghetti over a gas ring. They didn't say much. They just looked very natural together. Funny how you can tell when people are in love. Then I started to walk. I began to wonder what would happen if she left me. I'd have to find some way of earning a living to begin with. Suddenly I realized how much I'd grown to depend on her. All these expensive tastes I'd acquired while I was at the top—and now big tennis had finished with me—and so, apparently, had my wife. I can't ever remember being so scared. I dropped into a pub and had a few drinks. As I sat in the corner I thought of all sorts of things. . . . I thought of three different ways of killing him. I even thought of killing her. That seemed a far more sensible idea—and just as I was working out how I could do it—I suddenly saw something which completely changed my mind. (*Pause.*) I didn't go to that tournament after all. When I got back she was sitting exactly where you are now. I told her I'd decided to give up tennis and look after her instead. (*Pause.*)

LESGATE. Well?

TONY. (*Sharp change of mood, becomes cheerful.*) As things turned out—I needn't have got so worked up after all. Apparently that spaghetti evening had been a sort of fond farewell. The boy friend had been called back to New York.

LESGATE. An American?

TONY. Yes. There were long letters from there. . . . They usually arrived on Thursdays. She burnt all of them except one. That one she used to transfer from handbag to handbag. It was always with her. That letter became an obsession with me. I *had* to find out what was in it—and finally—I did. That letter made very interesting reading.

LESGATE. You mean you stole it?

TONY. Yes. I even wrote her two anonymous notes offering to sell it back.

LESGATE. Why?

TONY. I was hoping that would make her come and tell me all about him—but it didn't—so I kept the letter. (*Tony takes out wallet, and lets Max's letter fall out of it onto sofa. Lesgate picks it up and examines envelope.*)

LESGATE. Why are you telling me all this?

TONY. Because you're the only person I can trust. (*Lesgate puts the letter back in wallet and Tony snaps wallet shut.*) Anyway, that did it. It must have put the fear of God into them because the letters stopped—and we lived happily ever after. (*Changes tone.*) Funny to think that just a year ago I was sitting in that Knightsbridge pub—actually planning to murder her—and I might have done it if I hadn't seen something that changed my mind.

LESGATE. (*With back half turned to Tony—tapping pipe on ash tray on table back of sofa.*) Well. (*Tap—tap—tap.*) What did you see? (*Tap—tap.*)

TONY. (*Quietly, after short pause.*) I saw you. (*Long pause.*)

LESGATE. (*Turning round slowly to Tony.*) What was so odd about that?

TONY. The coincidence. You see only a week before I'd been to a reunion dinner and the fellows had been talking about you. How you'd been—court-martialed during the war—a year in prison! That was news. Mind you, at college we'd always said old Swann would end up in jail—that cash box, I suppose.

LESGATE. What about it?

TONY. (*With a laugh.*) My dear fellow, everybody knew you took that money. Poor old Alfred.

LESGATE. (*Rising.*) Well, thanks for the drink. Interesting hearing about your matrimonial affairs, I'm sure. (*Moving to hall.*) I take it you won't be wanting that car after all?

TONY. Don't you want me to tell you why I brought you here?

LESGATE. Yes, I think you'd better. (*During his following speech, Tony gets up from the sofa. He has dropped his limp. He takes out his handkerchief, wipes fingerprints off the reunion photograph and returns it to L. wall. Then he carefully wipes ash tray on coffee table, part of table and the brandy bottle. He crosses behind sofa—takes ash tray and dumps ashes into fireplace—again wipes with handkerchief and takes ash tray back to table behind sofa.*)

TONY. It was when I saw you in the pub that it happened. Suddenly everything became quite clear. Only a few months before, Margot and I had made our wills—quite short affairs leaving everything we had to each other in case of accidents. Hers worked out at just over ninety thousand pounds. Investments, mostly—all a little too easy to get at. And that was dangerous as they'd be bound to suspect me. I'd need an alibi—a very good one—and then I saw you. I'd often wondered what happened to people when they came out of prison—people like you, I mean. Can they get jobs? Do old friends rally round? Suppose they'd never had any friends. I was so curious to know that I followed you. I followed you home that night and—would you mind passing your glass? (*Lesgate, bewildered, hands Tony his glass.*) Thank you, thank you so much—and I've been following you ever since.
LESGATE. Why?
TONY. (*Wipes Lesgate's glass and puts it back on coffee table.*) I was hoping that, sooner or later, I might—catch you at something and be able to . . .
LESGATE. Blackmail me?
TONY. Influence you. After a few weeks I got to know your routine which made it a lot easier.
LESGATE. Rather dull work.
TONY. To begin with, yes. But you know how it is—you take up a hobby and the more you get to know of it the more fascinating it becomes. You became quite fascinating. In fact, there were times when I felt that you—almost belonged to me.
LESGATE. That must have been fascinating.
TONY. You always went dog-racing on Mondays and Thursdays. I even took it up myself—just to be near you. You'd changed your name to Adams.
LESGATE. Yes, I got bored with Swann. Any crime in that?
TONY. No, none at all. And you used to go to a little private club in Soho. It had an odd name . . . (*Remembering.*) The Kettle of Fish, that's it. The police closed it down recently, I believe—someone was caught taking drugs or something.
LESGATE. (*Casually.*) I never heard about that. J went there to eat. There's no crime in that either.
TONY. None whatever. In fact, there was nothing really illegal about you. I got quite discouraged, and then one day you disappeared from your lodgings, so I phoned your landlady. I said, "Mr.

Adams owed me five pounds." . . . Apparently that was nothing. Mr. Adams owed her six weeks' rent and her best lodger fifty-five pounds! And Mr. Adams had always been such a nice gentleman. That's what seemed to upset her most.

LESGATE. Yes, that's what always upsets them most. (*Lesgate strolls to coffee table and reaches for the brandy bottle.*)

TONY. (*Tony indicates gloves on arm of sofa.*) I say, old boy, if you want another drink, do you mind putting on these gloves? (*Lesgate glances at the gloves but does not pick them up.*) Thanks. Now, where were we? Oh, yes, I'd lost you and then I found you one day at the dog-racing and tailed you home to your new lodgings in Belsize Park. There Mr. Adams became Mr. Wilson. Mr. Wilson left Belsize Park last July owing fifteen weeks' rent and somewhat richer for his brief encounter with a . . . Miss Wallace. You used to go out with Miss Wallace on Wednesdays and Sundays. She certainly was in love with you, wasn't she? I suppose she thought you were growing that handsome mustache to please her. Poor Miss Wallace.

LESGATE. This is all most interesting. Do go on.

TONY. July—August—September . . . Apartment one two seven Carlisle Court . . . Occupant . . . A Mrs. Van Dorn. Her late husband left her two hotels and a large apartment house—furnished. What a base to operate from, Captain Lesgate! The only trouble is, she does rather enjoy being courted, and she is so very expensive. Perhaps that's why you've been trying to sell her car for over a month.

LESGATE. Mrs. Van Dorn asked me to sell it for her.

TONY. I know. I called her up just before you arrived here. She only wanted eight hundred. (*Pause. Lesgate remains perfectly still.*)

LESGATE. (*Casually.*) Where's the nearest police station?

TONY. Opposite the church. Two minutes' walk.

LESGATE. Suppose I walk there now?

TONY. What would you tell them?

LESGATE. Everything.

TONY. Everything? All about Mr. Adams and Mr. Wilson?

LESGATE. I shall simply tell them you are trying to blackmail me into . . .

TONY. Into?

LESGATE. Murdering your wife. (*Pause.*)

TONY. (*Amused.*) I almost wish you would. When she heard that we'd have the best laugh of our lives.

LESGATE. Aren't you forgetting something?

TONY. Am I?

LESGATE. You've told me a few things tonight.

TONY. What of it?

LESGATE. Suppose I tell them how you followed her to that studio in Chelsea—how you watched them cooking spaghetti and all that rubbish. Wouldn't that ring a bell?

TONY. It certainly would. They'd assume you followed her there yourself.

LESGATE. Me? Why should I?

TONY. Why should you steal her handbag? Why should you write her all those blackmail notes? Can you prove that you didn't? You certainly can't prove that I did. It will be a straight case of your word against mine.

LESGATE. (*Amused.*) Huh, that ought to puzzle them. What could you say?

TONY. I shall say that you came here tonight—half drunk—and tried to borrow money on the strength that we were at college together. When I refused you said something about a letter belonging to my wife. As far as I could make out you were offering to sell it to me. I gave you what money I had and you gave me the letter. It has your fingerprints on it. Remember? (*Takes wallet out of pocket and shows it to him.*) Then you said if I went to the police you'd tell some crazy story about my wanting you to murder my wife. But before we go any further, old boy—do consider the inconvenience. You see, I'm quite well known . . . and there would be pictures of you as well. Sooner or later a deputation of lodgers and landladies would come forward to testify to your character. And someone is almost certain to have seen you with Miss Wallace. (*Pause.*) You were always careful not to be seen around with her —I noticed. You usually met in out-of-the-way places where no one would recognize you—like that little tea shop in Pimlico.

LESGATE. That was her idea, not mine.

TONY. Yes, it was a bit crummy, wasn't it? Hardly a place to take Mrs. Van Dorn. By the way, does Mrs. Van Dorn know about —Mr. Adams—and Mr. Wilson . . . and Miss Wallace? You were planning to marry Mrs. Van Dorn, weren't you?

LESGATE. Smart, aren't you?

24

TONY. Not really, I've just had time to think things out—putting myself in your position. That's why I know you're going to agree.

LESGATE. What makes you *think* I'll agree?

TONY. For the same reason that a donkey with a stick behind him and a carrot in front goes forwards and not backwards. (*Long pause.*)

LESGATE. Tell me about the carrot. (*Long pause. Tony looks straight at Lesgate.*)

TONY. One thousand pounds in cash. (*Long pause. Lesgate looks up at Tony and their eyes meet.*)

LESGATE. For a murder?

TONY. For a few minutes' work. That's all it is. And no risk. I guarantee. That ought to appeal to you. You've been skating on very thin ice.

LESGATE. I don't know what you're talking about.

TONY. You should know. It was in all the papers. A middle-aged woman found dead due to an overdose of cocaine. Appeared as though she'd been taking the stuff for quite a time—but no one knows where she got it. . . . But we know—don't we? Poor Miss Wallace! (*This bites Lesgate and there is a long silence. Tony changes his tone.*) Yes, you should take a long holiday abroad. Surely a honeymoon with Mrs. Van Dorn would be preferable to ten years' detention at Dartmoor. My thousand pounds should see you safely married to her. You'll find it makes such a difference to have some money in the family.

LESGATE. This thousand pounds—where is it?

TONY. (*Quite serious.*) It's in a small attaché case in a check-room. (*Pause.*)

LESGATE. Where?

TONY. Somewhere in London. Of course, we don't meet again. As soon as you've—delivered the goods, I shall mail you the check-room ticket and the key to the case. (*Tony opens drawer in desk and, using his handkerchief, takes out a bundle of one-pound notes. He throws this across the room so that it lands on the sofa.*) You can take this hundred pounds on account. (*Lesgate looks down at the money but doesn't touch it.*)

LESGATE. (*Still skeptical.*) The police would only have to trace one of those notes back to you and they'd hang us from the same rope.

TONY. They won't. For a whole year I've been cashing an extra twenty pounds a week. Always in fivers. I then change them for these at my leisure.

LESGATE. (*Rises, crosses to desk.*) Let's see your bank statement.

TONY. By all means. (*Tony opens desk drawer and takes out his bank statement. He holds it open for Lesgate to see. Lesgate puts out his hands to touch it.*) Don't touch!

LESGATE. Turn back a page. (*Tony turns back the page.*) Your balance has dropped by over a thousand pounds in the year. Suppose the police ask you about that.

TONY. (*With a smile.*) I go dog-racing twice a week.

LESGATE. They'll check with your bookmaker?

TONY. Like you—I always bet on the Tote. . . . (*Pause.*) Satisfied? (*Long pause. Lesgate is standing R. of desk with back to windows. Tony faces him from other side of desk.*)

LESGATE. When would this take place?

TONY. Tomorrow night.

LESGATE. Tomorrow! Not a chance. I've got to think this over.

TONY. It's got to be tomorrow. I've arranged things that way.

LESGATE. Where?

TONY. Approximately where you're standing now. (*Lesgate reacts to this. A long pause.*)

LESGATE. (*Quietly.*) How?

TONY. Tomorrow evening, Halliday—that's the American boy friend—and I will go out to a stag party just down the road. She will stay here. She'll go to bed early and listen to Saturday Night Theater on the radio. She always does when I'm out. At exactly twenty-three minutes to eleven you will enter the house by the street door. (*Moving to hall.*) You'll find the key of this door under the stair carpet—here. (*Tony opens the hall door and leaves it wide open. He looks around to see that no one is watching and then points to one of the stairs which is clearly visible through the open door. He then comes in and closes the hall door.*)

LESGATE. The fifth step.

TONY. That's the one. Go straight to the window and hide behind the curtains. (*Pause.*) At exactly twenty minutes to eleven, I shall go to the telephone in the hotel to call my boss. I shall dial the wrong number—this number. That's all I shall do. (*Pause.*) When the phone rings you'll see the lights go on under the bedroom door. When she opens it the light will stream across the room, so don't move until she answers the phone. (*Pause.*) There must be as little

26

noise as possible. (*Pause.*) When you've finished, pick up the phone and give me a soft whistle. Then hang up. Don't speak, whatever you do. I shan't say a word. When I hear your whistle I shall hang up and redial—the *correct* number this time—I shall then speak to my boss as if nothing has happened and return to the party.

LESGATE. (*Looking round.*) What happens then? Go on! (*Tony points to leather suitcase resting on wall* L. *of* R. *bookcase.*)

TONY. You'll find this suitcase here. It will contain some clothes of mine for the cleaners. Open it and tip the clothes out onto the floor. (*Tony picks up the suitcase. He carries it back of couch to fireplace and puts it on the floor. He points to trophies on mantelpiece.*) Then fill it with the cigarette box and some of these cups. Close the lid but don't snap the locks. (*Pause.*) Then leave it here —just as it is now.

LESGATE. As if I left in a hurry?

TONY. That's the idea. Now—the window. If it's locked, unlock it and leave it open. (*Pause.*) Then go out exactly the same way as you came in.

LESGATE. (*Indicating hall door.*) By that door?

TONY. Yes—and here's the most important thing—as you go out, return the key to the place where you found it.

LESGATE. Under the stair carpet?

TONY. Yes. (*Lesgate looks round the room, puzzled.*)

LESGATE. Exactly what is supposed to have happened?

TONY. They'll assume you entered by the window. You thought the apartment was empty so you took the suitcase and went to work. She heard something and switched on her light. You saw the light go on under the door and hid behind the curtains. When she came in here you attacked her before she could scream. When you realized you'd actually killed her, you panicked and bolted into the garden leaving your loot behind.

LESGATE. Just a minute . . . I'm supposed to have entered by the windows. What if they had been locked?

TONY. It wouldn't matter. You see, she often takes a walk round the garden before she goes to bed and she usually forgets to lock up when she gets back. That's what I shall tell the police.

LESGATE. But she may say that . . . (*Pause.*)

TONY. She isn't going to say anything—is she? (*Pause, while Lesgate sees the logic of this.*)

27

LESGATE. Is there any reason why I shouldn't leave by the garden?

TONY. Yes. You'd have to climb an iron gate. If anyone saw you, you might be followed.

LESGATE. (*Turning to hall door.*) All right. I leave the flat—put the key back under the stair carpet, and go out by the street door. Suppose the street door's locked—how should I get in in the first place?

TONY. The street door's never locked.

LESGATE. When will you get back?

TONY. About twelve. I shall bring Halliday back for a nightcap— so we shall find her together. And we shall have been together since we left her—and there's my alibi. (*Lesgate looks round the room trying to visualize things. He moves slowly to hall door, opens it a few inches and peeps toward stairs. After a few seconds he closes it and turns to Tony.*)

LESGATE. You've forgotten something.

TONY. What?

LESGATE. When you return with—what's his name?—Halliday, how will you get into the apartment?

TONY. I shall let myself in.

LESGATE. But your key will be under the stair carpet. He's bound to see you take it out. That will give the whole show away. (*During Tony's speech Tony goes to hall door, wipes fingerprints off door handles, etc. Then crosses to desk and wipes desk and desk chair.*)

TONY. No, it won't be my key under the carpet. It will be hers. I shall take it from her handbag and hide it out there, just before I leave the flat. She won't be going out so she won't miss it. When I return with Halliday I'll use my own key to let us in. Then, while he's searching the garden or something, I'll take her key from under the stair carpet and return it to her handbag before the police arrive.

LESGATE. How many keys are there to that door?

TONY. Just hers and mine. (*The telephone rings. Tony hesitates, uncertain whether he should answer it. Then he goes to far side of desk so that he stands facing Lesgate with his back to the window. He picks up telephone. As soon as Tony answers phone, Lesgate picks up cotton gloves from arm of sofa and puts them on. He then moves around the room as follows: He opens the bedroom*

28

door and peers inside. He switches on bedroom light and, leaving bedroom door wide open, crosses to light switch and switches it off, then crosses and switches off standard lamp so that room is now lit only by the light from the bedroom. He crosses behind Tony to curtains and peers behind them. He draws the curtains aside. He unlocks the window, opens it and peers into the garden. He then opens and closes the window twice as if testing for a creak. He locks window and draws curtain shut. He switches on standard lamp and other lights and crosses to bedroom, switches off light and closes door. He then strolls to sofa and stares down at bundle of notes. He is doing this as Tony hangs up, i.e., finishes phone conversation. Telephone conversation—Tony and Margot. Her voice can be heard through receiver and she is gay and very happy.) Maida Vale 0401.

MARGOT. Tony, it's me.

TONY. *(Delighted.)* Hullo, darling! How's it going?

MARGOT. *(With great enthusiasm.)* Wonderfully! It's really a dreadful play—and we're enjoying every minute.

TONY. Oh—I'm sorry—I mean I'm glad.

MARGOT. How are you?

TONY. Very sleepy. *(Yawns.)* I've just made myself some coffee to try and keep awake. *(Tony sees Lesgate standing in bedroom doorway.)* Oh, darling, just a minute, I think there's someone at the door. *(To Lesgate, muffling telephone.)* Careful, you can be seen from the bedroom window. Sorry, darling, false alarm.

MARGOT. You will join us, won't you?

TONY. I'm afraid not—I hardly seem to have started.

MARGOT. *(Really disappointed.)* Oh, Tony! It never does work out, does it?

TONY. Oh, we'll manage it one day.

MARGOT. I say, darling . . .

TONY. Yes?

MARGOT. It seems awfully mean but—would you mind if Max and I went somewhere afterwards? You see . . .

TONY. Of course I don't mind. What do you want to do—dance?

MARGOT. Ummm!

TONY. Take him to Gerry's.

MARGOT. How do we get in?

TONY. Just mention my name. I don't know about the band but the food's good. By the way, Maureen rang up just after you left.

Wants us to go to dinner on Wednesday. You've got something down in your diary but I can't read your writing. (*He peers at the desk diary.*) Looks like Al—Bentall. Who's he? Another of your boy friends?

MARGOT. Albert Hall, you idiot!

TONY. Oh, the Albert Hall, of course. I'm so glad we can't go to Maureen's—she's such a filthy cook . . .

MARGOT. There's the bell—I must fly.

TONY. All right. 'Bye, sweet—enjoy yourself. (*Tony hangs up, then looks across at Lesgate.*) Well? (*Lesgate pauses undecided, then slowly picks up the notes and whisks them like a pack of cards. He looks up at Tony and places the notes in his inside pocket. Tony smiles.*)

CURTAIN

ACT II

The same. Saturday evening. The room is lit by the over-head lights and brackets. It is dark outside, the curtains are not drawn. The fire is burning brightly. The leather suitcase stands, as before, against wall L. of R. bookcase. Max's overcoat hangs on coat rack. Tony's raincoat is on hall chair. A small radio is on shelf of R. bookcase. Margot and Max are sitting on the sofa. She is showing him an album of press clippings. There are other clippings and folded newspapers on the coffee table in front of them. Tony is at drink shelf mixing drinks. Tony and Max wear dinner jackets. Margot is not wearing evening dress.

As the curtain rises they are all laughing.

TONY. . . . After that, he lost concentration and didn't win another game.

MARGOT. (*To Tony.*) Where's the picture of the Maharajah?

TONY. (*Moving behind sofa hands drink to Max.*) It's somewhere among those loose ones. (*Margot searches among clippings on coffee table. Tony, holding his drink, moves to fireplace and stands with back to fire. To Margot.*) Darling. When are you going to finish pasting in those press clippings?

MARGOT. I shall find time—one of these days. (*Unfolding piece of newspaper.*) Oh, here we are. (*Showing it to Max.*) There's the Maharajah. Isn't he dreamy?

TONY. He had four Rolls Royces and enough jewels to sink a battleship, but all he really wanted was to play at Wimbledon. (*Margot collects clippings from coffee table.*)

MARGOT. The poor darling. He was so short-sighted he could hardly see the end of his racket—let alone the ball.

MAX. (*Turning pages of album.*) You ought to write a book about all this. (*Max hands album to Margot. She puts the clippings inside it and lays it on the coffee table.*)

MARGOT. Why don't you two collaborate? A detective novel with a tennis background.

31

TONY. Murder on the center court . . . How about it, Max? Will you provide me with the perfect murder?

MAX. Nothing I'd like better.

TONY. How do you start to write a detective story?

MAX. Forget the detection and concentrate on crime. The crime's the thing. Imagine you're going to steal something, or murder somebody.

TONY. Is that what you do? Hmm! Interesting.

MAX. I always just put myself in the criminal's shoes and keep saying: "Well, what do I do next?"

MARGOT. (*To Max.*) Do you really believe in the perfect murder?

MAX. Absolutely—on paper. And I think I could plan one better than most people—but I doubt if I could carry it out.

TONY. Why not?

MAX. Because in stories things turn out as the author plans them to. . . . In real life they don't—always. (*He catches Margot's eye and they give each other a little smile.*) I imagine my murders would be rather like my bridge. . . . I'd make some damned stupid mistake and never realize it until I found that everyone was looking at me. (*Tony laughs and glances round at the clock on mantel.*)

TONY. I think we'd better drink up, Max. (*He finishes drink and crosses back of sofa to drink shelf.*)

MAX. All right, sir. (*He rises.*)

MARGOT. (*To Max.*) Are you doing anything tomorrow?

MAX. No. I don't think so.

MARGOT. (*To Tony.*) Why don't we all drive down to Windsor for lunch?

TONY. Good idea. (*To Max.*) Come along early. At least—not too early. We may be nursing a hangover. (*Tony crosses to stool.*)

MAX. About eleven?

TONY. (*To Max.*) That'll do fine. (*To Margot as he moves to hall.*) By the way, darling, did I lend you my latchkey? I can't find it anywhere.

MARGOT. (*Getting up.*) I may have them both in my handbag. I'll just look. (*Margot exits to bedroom. Max goes to hall to get his overcoat. Tony goes to French windows. He unlocks and opens a window and peers outside.*)

TONY. Raining pretty hard. I think I could lend you an old raincoat, if that's any good.

MAX. (*Taking down overcoat from coat rack.*) This will do. It isn't far, is it?

TONY. No—just around the corner. (*Tony glances round at Max to see if he is looking but he is putting on his overcoat and has his back to Tony. Tony deliberately opens one door of the French windows a few inches, draws the curtains across the windows. Margot enters from the bedroom carrying a handbag. She opens it and takes out a zip purse. Out of this she takes a latchkey.*)

MARGOT. I've only got one here. Are you sure yours isn't in your overcoat?

TONY. Yes, I've looked there. Could you lend me yours?

MARGOT. (*Holding key in hand.*) Well, that's a bit awkward.

TONY. (*Turning to Margot.*) Why?

MARGOT. I may want to go out. (*Pause.*)

TONY. Tonight?

MARGOT. Yes. I thought I might go to a movie or something.

TONY. But—aren't you going to listen to the radio—Saturday Night Theater?

MARGOT. (*Sitting on R. end of sofa.*) No, it's a thriller. I don't like thrillers when I'm alone.

TONY. (*Casually.*) I see. (*He goes and picks up raincoat on hall chair.*)

MARGOT. In any case I'll be back before you so I can let you in.

TONY. (*Putting on raincoat.*) We won't be back till after midnight. You may be asleep by then. (*He crosses to desk, taking gloves from raincoat pocket to put them on.*)

MAX. (*To Margot.*) You can always leave your key under the proverbial mat. (*Tony drops his key out of one of his gloves onto desk.*)

TONY. (*Picking it up.*) All right, chaps. Had it here in my glove all the time. (*Puts key back in raincoat pocket.*)

MARGOT. That settles that. (*She returns her key to her zip purse. She puts purse back in handbag, closes it and leaves it on oblong table behind sofa. NOTE: The back of the sofa must not obscure handbag from view.*)

TONY. What movie are you going to?

MARGOT. The Classic, I expect.

TONY. Will you get in? Saturday night.

MARGOT. I can always try. Now, don't make me stay in. You know how I hate doing nothing.

TONY. Nothing? But there're hundreds of things you can do. Have you written to Peggy about last week end? And what about these clippings? It's an ideal opportunity.

MARGOT. Well, I like that! You two go gallivanting while I have to stay in and do those boring clippings. (*Tony suddenly goes sullen.*)

TONY. Oh, very well then, we won't go. (*He moves L. above couch removing raincoat.*)

MARGOT. (*Astonished.*) What do you mean?

TONY. Well, it's quite obvious you don't want us to go out tonight—so we won't. We'll stay here with you. What shall we do—play cards? (*Puts raincoat on hall chair.*)

MARGOT. Now, Tony darling . . . (*She rises and goes to front of coffee table.*)

TONY. (*Going to phone.*) I'd better phone the Grendon and tell them we're not coming.

MARGOT. Tony, please. Don't let's be childish about this. I'll do your old press clippings.

TONY. (*Still sulking.*) You don't have to if you don't want to.

MARGOT. But I *do* want to. (*Margot picks up newspapers, press clippings and album from coffee table.*) Have we any paste?

TONY. There's some in the desk, I think.

MARGOT. Good. (*Takes album, newspapers and clippings to desk.*) And some scissors. In the mending basket. (*Tony goes to mending basket. He opens it, looks underneath a pair of Margot's stockings [show these] and takes out a long pair of scissors. Margot, taking out empty paste tube from desk drawer.*) Oh, look . . . the paste tube is empty. (*Exasperated.*) It would be. (*Tony stares at the empty paste tube which Margot is holding.*) Never mind. Mrs. Lucas is bound to have some.

TONY. Who's she?

MARGOT. She lives just across the road. I'll drop around later. (*Tony can't hide his annoyance. Margot reaches for scissors.*) Thank you, darling. (*Tony passes her scissors.*)

MAX. Why not make some? All you need is some flour and starch.

TONY. (*Pleased.*) Good idea. Do you know how to do it, Max?

MAX. (*Moving R. to kitchen.*) In two shakes. (*Max exits to kitchen.*)

TONY. Good old Max! (*To Margot.*) I'm sorry, darling. Was I very unreasonable?

34

MARGOT. (*Moving to Tony.*) No, I don't mind. I tell you what
. . . I'll paste these in tonight and you put up that extra shelf in
the kitchen . . . as you promised.
TONY. First thing tomorrow. Promise. (*He kisses her.*)
MAX. (*Calling from kitchen.*) Where's the starch?
MARGOT. I'll show you. (*Margot exits to kitchen. We can hear
them talking through the open door. Tony looks at oblong table
behind sofa. He glances quickly toward kitchen and then picks up
Margot's handbag and opens it. He takes out purse, zips it open
and takes out key and puts it on table. He then zips the purse shut,
returns it to handbag and closes bag, leaving it in exactly the same
position as before. He picks up key and goes and opens hall door,
leaving it wide open. He then looks along passage and to the landing above, then he lifts the stair carpet and places the key underneath. As he does this Margot gives a little peal of laughter from
the kitchen. Tony turns back, a little startled, as he strolls back
into the room, Margot enters from the kitchen with a cup and
spoon. Max follows her. As she is entering:*) It looks like vichy-
soisse without the chives.
MAX. If it starts to get thick, add a little water—and keep stirring.
(*Margot puts down cup on desk and starts to arrange the newspapers and clippings. Tony and Max stand in hall.*)
TONY. Keep the fire in for us, darling. (*He gets raincoat from
hall chair.*)
MARGOT. I will.
TONY. Oh, and it's just possible old man Burgess will phone to-
night. If he does, tell him I'm at the Grendon. It may be rather
important.
MARGOT. What's the number?
TONY. It's in the book.
MARGOT. All right. Well, look after each other.
MAX. We will. Good night, Margot.
MARGOT. 'Night, Max. (*To Tony.*) You'll run Max home in the
car afterwards, won't you, darling?
TONY. Of course. We'll drop in here first for a nightcap. Sure
you won't be up?
MARGOT. I shall be fast asleep. And I *don't* want to be disturbed.
TONY. Then we'll be as quiet as mice. (*Tony kisses Margot*)
Good night, darling.
MARGOT. Good night.

35

TONY. Come on, Max. (*They exit through hall door, closing it. Margot switches on lamp, turns on radio. Then she turns off chandelier and brackets. She turns to her work at desk. She looks resigned to it. She unfolds a piece of newspaper, picks up scissors, starts cutting. Music swells to:*)

CURTAIN

ACT II

SCENE 2

The same. Later that night. Margot has finished pasting in Tony's press clippings and has left the album lying open on the desk. By the album lie some pieces of newspaper and the scissors. The wastepaper basket is overflowing with cut pieces of newspaper. Margot's handbag is still on the table behind sofa.

When the curtain rises the room is lit only by the light from the fire which is still burning well. After a few seconds the hall door opens, but only about two inches, as if someone was listening. Another few seconds and Lesgate enters. He stands in the doorway perfectly still—listening. He wears a raincoat and kid gloves but no hat. He closes the door without a sound except for the final click as it locks. As he crosses silently he takes off his scarf and ties two knots in it. [NOTE: This scarf must have tassel ends, to emphasize, later, that it is a scarf and must be silk and tan colored so that Margot could mistake it for a stocking.] Lesgate crosses to French windows. The phone rings. He quickly hides behind curtains. After some time the light goes on under the bedroom door and Margot enters from the bedroom. She leaves the door wide open and the light is thrown across the room. Margot puts on a dressing gown as she crosses to the telephone. She goes to the far side of the desk and answers the phone with her back turned to the window.

MARGOT. Hullo. . . . (*She listens for several seconds then louder.*) Hullo! (*Margot does not notice Lesgate as he comes from*

36

behind the curtains. *His gloved hands hold each end of the silk scarf in which two knots have been tied. Margot has had the phone in her left hand. She puts phone hand down and jiggles the receiver with her right. Just as she is jiggling the receiver Lesgate attacks her, throwing the scarf over her head and drawing it back sharply against her throat. With a strangled gurgle she drops the phone. Lesgate holds her back against his body but Margot's hands catch hold of the scarf and try to tear it away. They struggle for a moment, then Lesgate winds the scarf, with his left hand, right around her neck and at the same time she turns round so that she faces him with the scarf crossed at the back of her neck. He pushes her against the end of the desk and forces her down until she is bent right back along the top of the desk with her head downstage.* [NOTE: *To avoid hurting her back Margot should sit on end of desk before lying back.*])

(*In his efforts to tighten the scarf he leans right over her so that his body almost touches hers. Margot's right hand leaves the scarf and waves over the end of the desk, groping for the scissors. She grabs them and strikes with one of the points into Lesgate's back. Lesgate slumps over her and then very slowly rolls over the left side of the desk, landing on his back with a strangled grunt. Margot continues to lie back over the desk, completely exhausted. Then she manages to get to her feet, all the time fighting for breath. She tears the scarf away from her throat but it remains looped around her shoulders. She grabs the telephone. At first she has difficulty in speaking. A sharp "Hello" from Tony can be heard from the receiver.*)

TONY. Hullo!

MARGOT. (*In short gasps.*) Get the police—quickly—police!

TONY. Margot.

MARGOT. Who's that?

TONY. Darling, it's me . . .

MARGOT. Oh, thank God—Tony, come back at once.

TONY. What's the matter?

MARGOT. (*Panicking.*) I can't explain now. Come quickly—please!

TONY. (*Angrily.*) Darling, pull yourself together. . . . What is it?

MARGOT. (*Recovering slightly.*) A man—attacked me . . . tried to strangle me . . .

37

TONY. Has he gone?

MARGOT. No—he's dead . . . he's dead . . . (*A long pause.*) Tony—Tony. Are you still there?

TONY. (*Frozen.*) Margot.

MARGOT. Yes?

TONY. Now, listen very carefully.

MARGOT. Yes, I'm listening.

TONY. Don't touch anything. I'll be with you in a minute.

MARGOT. No, I won't.

TONY. Don't touch anything and don't speak to anybody—until I get back.

MARGOT. All right. I won't touch anything.

TONY. You promise?

MARGOT. (*In angry panic.*) Yes, I promise—only please be quick! (*She begins to sob with fright as she replaces the phone. She staggers to window and opens it, goes outside. After several seconds she returns, having left scarf outside. The windows remain open. As she reaches desk and sees the body, she starts to hall door, stops and collapses on hall chair, sobs, then exits into bedroom and locks door. A few seconds pause. Chimes are heard from church clock outside. Another short pause. Sound of street door opening. Running footsteps in passage outside apartment. Sound of key in lock, hall door opens. Tony switches on wall bracket lights only. He takes in situation, stares at body, then at handbag and back to body, then he takes key out of door, puts it in raincoat pocket. He closes door quietly. He turns on standard lamp. He crosses to Lesgate and starts to examine body, curious to see how he died. He turns body half over and sees scissors in back. (NOTE: Unless trick-scissors are used, turn body away from audience so they would not see scissors.) He glances at hands for blood and then glances at bedroom door. Searches for key in Lesgate's pockets. He can't find it. Sound of bedroom door unlocking. Tony rises and Margot comes rushing into his arms.*) Oh, Tony, Tony, Tony . . .

TONY. It's all right—it'll be all right. What happened? (*Margot clings like a frightened child. Tony lifts her head slightly so he can see her throat.*)

MARGOT. He got something around my throat—it felt like a stocking.

TONY. Are you sure? Let me see. (*He touches her throat gently and she turns her head away quickly.*) I'd better call a doctor.

MARGOT. (*Shocked at the thought.*) But he's dead.

TONY. (*Glancing at body.*) I know. When he fell he must have driven those scissors right through himself.

MARGOT. (*Turning away.*) Horrible! Can't you . . .?

TONY. Yes—right away. (*Tony exits quickly into bedroom. Margot suddenly puts her hand to her head. She turns and looks round the room. She sees her handbag on the sofa table, opens it, and fishes around inside. Tony enters from the bedroom carrying a blanket. When he sees what Margot is doing he stops dead and stares at her in horror.*) What are you doing?

MARGOT. (*Taking out a bottle of aspirin.*) Will you get me some water, please? (*Margot drops the handbag onto the sofa table. Tony fills a glass with water from the drink shelf and hands it to Margot who swallows some aspirin and takes a drink. Tony throws the blanket over Lesgate.*)

TONY. (*Quietly.*) That's better. (*He covers the body.*)

MARGOT. Shut the window, please.

TONY. No—we mustn't touch anything until the police arrive. (*Looking at open window.*) He must have broken in. (*Looking around room.*) I wonder what he was after? (*Looking at silver cups.*) Those cups, I expect.

MARGOT. When will the police get here?

TONY. (*Startled.*) Have you called them already?

MARGOT. No. You told me not to speak to anyone. Hadn't you better call them now?

TONY. (*Pause.*) Yes, in a minute.

MARGOT. (*Moving to bedroom.*) I'll get dressed.

TONY. Why?

MARGOT. They'll want to see me.

TONY. They're not going to see you.

MARGOT. But they'll have to ask me questions.

TONY. They can wait until tomorrow. I'll tell them all they want to know. (*As Tony is speaking he keeps looking around the desk, searching for something. Margot moves to bedroom door and then turns.*)

MARGOT. Tony.

TONY. Yes?

MARGOT. Why did you phone me? (*Tony stares back at her for at least three seconds before answering.*)

TONY. What? Er—sorry—I'll tell you about that later. (*Changing*

39

the subject.) I just thought of something. You said he used a stocking . . .

MARGOT. I think it was a stocking—or a scarf. Isn't it there?

TONY. (*Looking around.*) No. But I expect they'll find it. Now you get back to bed. I'll phone them right away. (*Tony goes over to Lesgate. Searches for key, finds it in raincoat pocket. Sighs with relief. Goes back to sofa table and returns key carefully to zip purse and closes handbag. Sighs with relief again. Returns to body and covers it with blanket. Then goes to phone and dials. Margot appears in bedroom door.*)

MARGOT. Where's Max, Tony?

TONY. I told him to go straight home. . . . Hello, Operator— give me the Maida Vale Police quickly. . . .

MARGOT. Did you tell him?

TONY. No. I wasn't sure what had happened, so I just said I was feeling rotten. . . . Darling . . . go back to bed and . . . (*Margot exits and closes her door.*)

POLICE. (*Offstage, heard through receiver.*) Maida Vale Police.

TONY. Police? There's been a ghastly accident.

POLICE. Yes, sir?

TONY. A man has been killed.

POLICE. Your name, sir?

TONY. Wendice.

POLICE. (*Spelling.*) D I double S . . .?

TONY. No. D I C E.

POLICE. Your address, sir?

TONY. 61a Charrington Gardens. It's the ground-floor apartment.

POLICE. When was this accident?

TONY. About ten minutes ago. He broke in and attacked my wife . . .

POLICE. A burglar?

TONY. (*Impatiently.*) Yes. I'll explain everything when you get here. How long will that take?

POLICE. About two minutes.

TONY. Two minutes.

POLICE. Don't touch anything, will you, sir?

TONY. No. We won't touch anything. Good-bye. (*He hangs up and looks around the room. Finally he goes to open window and steps out. Stoops down and picks something up. Comes back into room. He is holding each end of Lesgate's scarf with the two knots.*

*Strolls thoughtfully to mending basket, searches in it and finds a
stocking. He holds up scarf and stocking, comparing them. Then he
drops stocking on stool and hides scarf in his pocket. He then
kneels down beside Lesgate and takes out his wallet.)*

MARGOT. (*Off, sharply.*) Tony!

TONY. (*Calling back.*) All right, darling. Won't be a minute.
(*Tony takes letter [Max's] out of his wallet, using his handkerchief,
and starts to put it in Lesgate's pocket. . . .)*

CURTAIN

ACT II

SCENE 3

The same. Sunday morning. About 11 A. M.

*The curtains are drawn open and it is bright and sunny
outside. The wastepaper basket has been emptied. Lesgate's body has been removed but the blanket, folded
once, still lies on the desk over "the spot" to hide blood
stains. The fire is out and has not been touched since last
night. The dirty breakfast things lie on the coffee table.
Margot is still very nervous. She stands C. as curtain rises.*

MARGOT. More coffee?

TONY. (*Off L.*) No, thank you. (*Enters from bedroom tying tie,
goes to front of fireplace.*)

MARGOT. We'd better call Max—(*Quietly.*)—and tell him.

TO. JY. I have. He's on his way over.

MARGOT. (*Trying to cheer up.*) Did he like the party last night?

TONY. He certainly did. Made a remarkably good speech, except
that he would keep referring to us as Limies. (*He laughs.*) Oh,
yes, he's all there, is Max. . . . Where did you dig him up?
(*Pause.*)

MARGOT. I—met him at Peggy's once—and then I met him again
just before he went back to New York.

TONY. (*Lightly.*) Oh, yes—so you told me. (*Pause.*)

MARGOT. Tony, why did you . . .? } (*Together.*)
TONY. By the way, I . . .

TONY. Sorry.

MARGOT. No, go on.

TONY. I've closed the shutters in the bedroom, that's all.

MARGOT. (*Anxiously.*) Why?

TONY. People have started to go out for their Sunday papers. We now have a collection of refined snoopers.

MARGOT. How awful! Is it in the papers already?

TONY. I don't think so—not yet. But news travels fast. (*Pause.*) What were you going to say?

MARGOT. I—can't remember—it's gone for the moment. (*The phone rings. Margot gives a nervous start. Tony answers it.*)

TONY. Hullo.

REPORTER. (*Offstage, heard through receiver.*) Mrs. Wendice, please.

TONY. This is Mr. Wendice.

REPORTER. Oh, good morning, sir. I'm with the C. & S. News Service. Might I see Mrs. Wendice for a few minutes?

TONY. I'm afraid my wife can't see anyone just now—not for a day or two.

REPORTER. Oh. Was she hurt in any way?

TONY. No. She's all right now.

REPORTER. I just want one or two photographs.

TONY. No—I'm afraid . . .

REPORTER. But surely . . .

TONY. (*Suddenly annoyed.*) I'm sorry—good-bye. (*Tony rings off.*)

MARGOT. Who was that?

TONY. Just a reporter—wanted to take some photographs of you.

MARGOT. I suppose we shall get a lot of that.

TONY. Not for long. As soon as the inquest's over they'll forget all about it. . . . So will you.

MARGOT. When will it be?

TONY. The inquest? Tomorrow or Tuesday—I should think.

MARGOT. (*Nervously.*) What will happen?

TONY. Nothing to worry about. The coroner will probably congratulate you for putting up such a good show.

MARGOT. For killing a man?

TONY. Now don't start getting ideas about that. It was him or you. As the police surgeon said, it was lucky those scissors were on the desk.

MARGOT. Why were the police so long last night?

TONY. Were they? I didn't notice. I'm afraid I dropped off to sleep very quickly.

MARGOT. I know you did. They stayed for hours. Cars seemed to be coming and going all night.

TONY. I only saw the sergeant. Nice chap. He seemed to have it all under control.

MARGOT. At one time I thought they must be turning all the furniture round.

TONY. (*Looking around the room.*) Well, they haven't made much mess. They've even emptied the wastepaper basket. That was thoughtful of them.

MARGOT. Someone kept flashing a light under the bedroom door.

TONY. Taking photographs, probably.

MARGOT. About two o'clock I couldn't stand it any longer. I got up and came in here.

TONY. (*Surprised.*) You came in here? What for?

MARGOT. To ask them when they expected to finish. But when I saw them I—couldn't say anything. Two men were on the floor with a tape measure. Another was outside. He kept opening and shutting the window. They all stopped what they were doing and looked at me. I felt such a fool. (*Slowly.*) And on the desk—were a pair of shoes. . . . His, I suppose. (*Putting hand to head.*) It was horrible! (*Tony has remembered something.*)

TONY. Darling—before I forget—the sergeant wanted to know why you didn't phone the police immediately.

MARGOT. (*Flustered.*) But how could I? You were on the phone.

TONY. I know, but . . .

MARGOT. (*Agitated.*) You distinctly told me not to speak to anyone until you got here.

TONY. I know, darling. But I told him a slightly different story.

MARGOT. Why?

TONY. (*Slowly.*) I said that you didn't call the police because you naturally assumed that I would phone them from the hotel. (*Pause.*)

MARGOT. Why did you say that?

TONY. Because—it was the perfectly logical explanation—and he accepted it. You see, if they got the idea that we had delayed reporting it—even for a few minutes—they might get nosy and start asking a lot of questions and . . .

MARGOT. So you want me to say the same thing?

TONY. I think so. (*Doorbell rings.*) Just in case it comes up again. I expect that's Max. Let him in, will you, darling? I'll just get rid of these. (*Tony exits into kitchen with tray of dishes. Margot goes to hall door and opens it. Detective Inspector Hubbard is standing in the passage outside.*)

HUBBARD. (*Removing hat.*) Good morning, madam.

MARGOT. Oh! Good morning.

HUBBARD. Mrs. Wendice?

MARGOT. Yes.

HUBBARD. I'm a police officer. (*Pause.*) May I come in?

MARGOT. Of course. (*Nervously.*) Excuse me, I'll tell my husband you're here.

HUBBARD. Thank you. (*Margot exits to kitchen. Hubbard looks around for a place to hang his hat. He sees coat rack by the door and hangs it up. He then strolls into the room and looks the place over, getting his bearings. He glances from the blanket to the window, to the telephone, to the bedroom door. He then looks around until he sees the mending basket. Tony and Margot enter from kitchen.*)

TONY. Good morning.

HUBBARD. Good morning, sir. I'm Chief Inspector Hubbard. I'm in charge of the Criminal Investigation of this division.

TONY. I think I gave your sergeant all the necessary information.

HUBBARD. Yes, I've seen his report, of course, but there are a few things I'd like to get first hand. I gather my sergeant only saw you for a few moments, Mrs. Wendice? (*Turning suddenly to Margot.*) Mrs. Wendice?

MARGOT. Yes . . . I . . .

TONY. My wife was suffering from considerable shock.

HUBBARD. (*Sympathetically.*) Yes, that was a very nasty experience you had. (*Turning to bedroom door.*) Mind if I take a look around?

TONY. Go ahead. The bedroom and bathroom are through here. . . . (*Tony follows Hubbard into the bedroom. Margot starts to follow them, then hangs back. She is now very nervous. She looks at the blanket on the desk and stares at it for a moment. Then she goes to the cigarette box on the table behind sofa, opens it, takes out a cigarette, fingers it and then puts it back again. Hubbard and Tony enter from bedroom.*)

HUBBARD. Well, he certainly didn't get in by the bathroom

44

TONY. And the kitchen has bars on the window. (*Tony opens the kitchen door. Hubbard glances in for a moment and then comes back into the room.*) We assume he must have come in through these windows.

HUBBARD. Hmmm. I understand that you weren't here when this happened, sir?

TONY. No. I was at a dinner party at the Grendon Hotel.

HUBBARD. Just down the road?

TONY. Yes. By a curious coincidence I was actually phoning my wife when she was attacked.

HUBBARD. So I gather. Can you tell me exactly what time it was?

TONY. I—I'm not sure.

HUBBARD. Did you notice—Mrs. Wendice?

MARGOT. No, I didn't.

HUBBARD. You phoned the police at three minutes to eleven, sir.

TONY. Let me see—in that case it must have been—about a quarter to eleven. By the way—won't you sit down, Inspector? (*Tony waves Hubbard to the sofa. Tony brings the stool to sofa and sits. Margot and Hubbard sit on sofa, Hubbard between Margot and Tony.*)

HUBBARD. Thank you.

MARGOT. Have you any idea who he was?

HUBBARD. Yes. At least we've discovered where he lived. There still seems to be some confusion as to his real name.

MARGOT. Oh?

HUBBARD. He appeared to have several. (*Suddenly, looking at Margot.*) Had you ever seen him before?

MARGOT. (*Bewildered.*) Why—no, of course not. (*Hubbard takes out his notebook and produces two snapshots of different sizes. He hands them to Margot, one by one, and watches her very closely as she glances at them and hands them back.*) Oh, is this —him?

HUBBARD. Yes. You don't recognize him?

MARGOT. No. I—I never saw him.

HUBBARD. Didn't you even—catch a glimpse of his face?

MARGOT. No. You see, he attacked me from behind and it was dark. I hardly saw him at all.

HUBBARD. (*Pleasantly.*) But before I showed you those photographs, you said you'd never seen him before. (*A pause, he*

45

watches her face.) How could you know that—if you never saw his face last night? (*Pause.*)

MARGOT. I don't quite understand. . . .

TONY. (*Interrupting.*) Inspector, my wife simply meant that, as far as she knew, she had never seen him before.

HUBBARD. (*To Margot.*) Was that what you meant?

MARGOT. (*Nervously.*) Yes—I'm sorry.

HUBBARD. How about you, sir? Ever seen him before? (*Hubbard hands Tony one of the photographs. Tony looks and hands it back.*)

TONY. No. (*Hubbard hands him the other. Tony looks at it.*) No . . . (*He starts to hand it back.*) At least . . . (*Taking another look.*)

HUBBARD. Yes?

TONY. (*Amazed.*) It's very like someone I was at college with—the mustache makes quite a difference.

HUBBARD. What was his name?

TONY. Now you're asking. . . . It's nearly twenty years since I left.

HUBBARD. Was it Lesgate?

TONY. No.

HUBBARD. Wilson?

TONY. No.

HUBBARD. Swann?

TONY. No . . . Swann? Wait a minute—Swann . . . Yes, that's it. (*Crosses back of sofa, gets photo off L. wall and brings it to Hubbard.*) Look, here's an old photo taken at a reunion dinner. We were at the same college. There he is—it's unbelievable!

HUBBARD. Did you know him well?

TONY. No. He was senior to me.

HUBBARD. Have you met him since then?

TONY. No—at least—come to think of it, I did see him—quite recently (*Pause.*) but not to speak to.

HUBBARD. When was that?

TONY. About six months ago. It was at a railway station. . . . Waterloo, I think. I remember noticing how little he'd changed.

HUBBARD. Had he a mustache then?

TONY. (*Pauses for thought, then hands photo back to Hubbard.*) No. (*Hubbard makes a note of this. Then he turns to Margot.*)

46

HUBBARD. (*Getting up.*) Mrs. Wendice, would you show me exactly what happened last night?

MARGOT. Tony, do I have to?

TONY. Afraid so, darling. (*Tony helps her up. As she talks Margot crosses to bedroom and then back of sofa to c. and then to phone.*)

MARGOT. I was in bed when the phone rang. I got up and came in here.

HUBBARD. Did you switch this light on?

MARGOT. No.

HUBBARD. Just show me exactly where you were standing. (*Margot stands at desk as she did, with back half-turned to window.*)

MARGOT. I stood here. I picked up the phone.

HUBBARD. Are you sure you had your back to the window like that?

MARGOT. Yes.

HUBBARD. But why?

MARGOT. (*Bewildered.*) Why not? (*Hubbard stands at L of desk facing window.*)

HUBBARD. Why go around the desk? I should have picked it up from this side. (*Hubbard picks up the phone with right hand and then replaces it.*)

TONY. Surely my wife can remember . . .

HUBBARD. Just a moment, sir.

MARGOT. But I always answer the phone from here.

HUBBARD. Why?

MARGOT. So that if I want to write anything down—I can hold the phone in my left hand. (*She places her left hand on the phone.*)

HUBBARD. I see. All right—go on.

MARGOT. I picked up the phone. Then he must have come from behind the curtain and attacked me. He got something round my neck . . .

HUBBARD. Something? What do you mean by "something"?

MARGOT. I think it was a stocking.

HUBBARD. I see. What happened then?

MARGOT. He pushed me over the desk. I remember distinctly feeling for the scissors . . .

HUBBARD. Where were those scissors usually kept?

MARGOT. (*Pointing.*) In that mending basket. I'd forgotten to put them away.

HUBBARD. Now what makes you think he came from behind those curtains?

MARGOT. Where else could he have been?

HUBBARD. The curtains were drawn, I suppose?

MARGOT. Yes, they were.

HUBBARD. Did you draw them yourself?

TONY. (*A little weary of all this.*) I drew them, Inspector—before I went out.

HUBBARD. Did you lock the window at the same time?

TONY. Yes.

HUBBARD. Are you quite sure of that, sir?

TONY. Perfectly sure. I always lock up when I draw the curtains.

HUBBARD. Then how do you suppose he got into this room?

TONY. We assumed—that he broke in.

HUBBARD. There's no sign of a break-in. The lock's quite un-damaged.

TONY. But he must have done. When I got back that window was wide open. At least . . . Margot, are you sure you didn't go out into the garden last night and forget to lock up afterwards?

MARGOT. I did go out for a moment. After—after he attacked me. I wanted to get some air. I pushed the window open and stood on the terrace outside.

HUBBARD. Did you call for help?

MARGOT. I'd just spoken to my husband on the telephone.

HUBBARD. You say you pushed the window open. Are you sure you didn't unlock it first?

MARGOT. Yes. Quite sure.

HUBBARD. Was it already open?

MARGOT. I—I—don't remember. (*Pause.*)

HUBBARD. Mrs. Wendice, why didn't you ring the police immediately this happened? (*Tony catches Margot's eye and she looks at him for a moment.*)

MARGOT. (*Trying to remember what Tony told her.*) I was trying to get through—to the police when I discovered that my husband was on the line. (*Pause.*) I naturally thought he would call the police—from the hotel—before he came here. (*Pause. Tony looks relieved.*)

HUBBARD. (*Quietly.*) Didn't it occur to you to call—for a doctor?

MARGOT. No.

HUBBARD. Why ever not?

MARGOT. He was—dead.

HUBBARD. (Quietly.) How did you know that?

MARGOT. I—it was obvious.

HUBBARD. Did you feel his pulse?

MARGOT. No—of course I didn't. Anyone would have realized he was dead. . . . One look at those staring eyes . . .

HUBBARD. (Accusingly.) So you did see his face, after all?

MARGOT. (Losing control.) I saw his eyes. I can't remember his face.

TONY. Inspector, my wife has obviously never seen this man before. And if he didn't get in by those windows—how did he get in? (Hubbard strolls across to hall door.)

HUBBARD. (Slowly.) As a matter of fact we're quite certain he came in by this door. (Hubbard opens it a few inches and closes it with a click. Then he looks across at Tony.)

MARGOT. (Quietly.) But it was locked.

TONY. Margot, did you open this door at all—and forget to close it after we'd gone?

MARGOT. No.

HUBBARD. How many keys are there to this door?

MARGOT. Only two. Mine was in my handbag and (To Tony.) you had yours with you.

TONY. That's right.

HUBBARD. Has the caretaker got a key?

MARGOT. No.

HUBBARD. (To Margot.) Do you employ a charwoman?

MARGOT. Yes, but she hasn't got one, either. I'm always in when she comes.

TONY. What makes you think he came in that way?

HUBBARD. (Quite simply.) His shoes.

TONY. His shoes? (Hubbard crosses to window.)

HUBBARD. The ground was soaking wet last night. If he'd come in by the garden he'd have left marks all over the carpet. (Pause.) He didn't leave any because he wiped his shoes on the front door mat.

TONY. How can you tell?

HUBBARD. It's a fairly new mat and some of its fibers came off on his shoes. . . .

TONY. But surely . . .

HUBBARD. And there was a small tar stain on the mat and some of the fibers show that as well. There's no question about it.

TONY. (Suddenly.) Wait a minute, I think I've got it. (To Margot.) You remember when your bag was stolen?

MARGOT. Yes.

TONY. Wasn't your key inside?

MARGOT. Yes, but it was still there when I got it back.

HUBBARD. (Interested.) Just a moment. I'd like to hear about this. What sort of bag?

TONY. A handbag, Inspector. My wife lost it at Victoria Station.

MARGOT. I got it back from the lost and found office about two weeks later.

HUBBARD. Was anything missing?

MARGOT. All the money had gone.

HUBBARD. Anything else? (Margot seems uncertain what to say.)

MARGOT. No.

HUBBARD. (Casually.) No papers—or letters?

MARGOT. No.

HUBBARD. (With sudden emphasis.) Are you quite sure about that?

MARGOT. (Determined.) Yes.

HUBBARD. And your latchkey was in your handbag when you lost it?

MARGOT. Yes, but it was still there when it was returned.

TONY. Whoever stole that money could have had the key copied.

HUBBARD. Where was the bag found eventually?

MARGOT. At Victoria Station.

TONY. But not until several days later. By which time he could have had a duplicate made and returned the original to the bag.

HUBBARD. Before you go any further with this—how did he get in through the street door?

TONY. The street door's always unlocked.

HUBBARD. I see. He could have had your key copied. And he could have used it to open this door—but of course, he didn't.

TONY. Why not?

HUBBARD. Because if he had—the key would still have been on him when he died. But no key was found when we went through his pockets. (Pause.)

TONY. I see. Well—we seem to be back where we started.

50

HUBBARD. Not quite. (*Pause.*) You said you saw this man at Waterloo Station?

TONY. Yes.

HUBBARD. Are you sure it wasn't—Victoria? (*Tony thinks for a moment.*)

TONY. It may have been. (*Turning to Margot excitedly.*) When did you lose the bag? Wasn't it that week end when we went to Peggy's? Yes, it was. It was Victoria. I remember now. He was sitting in the restaurant when I saw him.

HUBBARD. (*To Margot.*) And was that where you left your handbag?

TONY. Yes, it was. (*To Margot.*) You were with me, of course—didn't I say something about—there's someone I was at college with?

MARGOT. I don't remember. (*Tony looks at Hubbard who looks at Margot.*)

HUBBARD. It looks as if he may have had something to do with that handbag, after all. The next thing is to get all this down on paper. I'd like you both to make an official statement before the inquest. (*Pause.*) My office is only a few minutes from here. Perhaps you could come now? (*The doorbell rings.*)

TONY. Excuse me. (*Tony opens hall door and Max enters.*)

MAX. Hullo, Tony. (*Max goes to Margot and then notices Hubbard.*) Margot . . .

TONY. Max, this is Inspector Hubbard. This is Mr. Halliday, Inspector. He was with me last night.

MAX. How do you do? (*Bewildered.*)

HUBBARD. Mr. Halliday, as you were with Mr. Wendice last night, you may be able to help us here. Did you notice what time it was when he went to the phone? (*Max thinks for a moment.*)

MAX. Yes—it was about twenty to eleven.

HUBBARD. (*Making note.*) How did you come to notice that?

MAX. Well, when Mr. Wendice got up from the table I thought for a moment we were leaving the party, so I looked at my watch.

HUBBARD. Thank you, sir. You see, it was when Mrs. Wendice came in here to answer his call that she was attacked.

MAX. You mean (*To Tony.*) you were phoning Margot . . .?

TONY. Yes.

MAX. But I don't get this. I asked you if we were leaving and you said you were just going out to phone . . . your boss . . .

51

MARGOT. (Suddenly, turning to Tony.) Tony, I know what I was going to ask you. Why did you phone me last night? (All turn on Tony.)

HUBBARD. (Crossing to Tony.) Now, just a moment. Before I lose the thread of this. At about twenty to eleven you left your party to phone your boss?

TONY. Yes. I used the pay phone in the lobby.

HUBBARD. Now, how long were you on the phone to your boss before you called your wife?

TONY. As a matter of fact I never did speak to him. I couldn't remember his number—so I rang my wife to ask her to look it up in the address book on the desk.

MARGOT. You mean you hauled me out of bed just to give you his phone number?

TONY. I had to. (To Hubbard.) My boss was flying to Brussels this morning and I wanted to remind him of something. It was rather important.

HUBBARD. Wasn't there a telephone directory in the hotel?

TONY. (Calmly.) Yes, but he was at home—his home number isn't listed.

HUBBARD. So you never called him, after all?

TONY. No. Naturally when I heard what had happened here—I forgot all about it.

HUBBARD. I see. (To Max.) Mr. Halliday, Mr. and Mrs. Wendice are coming to my office now to make their statements. (Taking out notebook.) Would you give me your address, sir? I may want to get in touch with you. (Tony goes out by hall door.)

MAX. Certainly.

MARGOT. I'll get my coat. (She exits into bedroom.)

MAX. I'm staying at the Carfax Hotel. . . .

HUBBARD. (Handing Max notebook and pencil.) Just write it down there, will you? Telephone number as well. (Watching Max write.) Ever been over here before, sir? (Max doesn't see the catch in this.)

MAX. (Writing.) Yes, about a year ago.

HUBBARD. Umhm. (Max hands notebook to Hubbard who glances at address and returns it to his pocket. Tony enters by hall door.)

TONY. Inspector, there's a devil of a crowd outside. Can't you send them away?

HUBBARD. They'll come back faster than they go, sir. I was going to suggest we left by the garden. Isn't there a gate at the far end?

TONY. Yes, but it may still be locked. I'll just see. (*Tony unlocks window and exits into garden. Hubbard waits till he has gone and then turns to Max.*)

HUBBARD. (*Confidentially.*) How much does he know—about you and Mrs. Wendice?

MAX. (*Startled.*) What are you talking about?

HUBBARD. You wrote a letter to Mrs. Wendice—from New York. (*Max only stares at Hubbard.*) It was found in the dead man's inside pocket. I didn't mention it because I wasn't sure how much Mr. Wendice knew. Have you any idea how it got there?

MAX. No. (*Margot enters from bedroom. She is wearing an over coat and carries her handbag.*)

MARGOT. Where's Tony?

MAX. He's just gone into the garden.

HUBBARD. Mrs. Wendice. When you lost your handbag, did you lose a letter as well? (*Margot looks quickly at Max.*)

MARGOT. No.

MAX. Margot, it was found in this man's pocket.

HUBBARD. You did lose it—didn't you? (*Pause.*)

MARGOT. Yes, I did.

HUBBARD. I asked you that before, didn't I?

MARGOT. Yes—but you see—my husband didn't know about it.

HUBBARD. This man was blackmailing you, wasn't he? (*No reply.*)

MAX. It's no good, Margot. Tony will have to know about it now. (*Max takes out his wallet. Margot stares at him horrified.*)

MARGOT. No!

MAX. It's the only thing to do. Inspector, after Mrs. Wendice lost my letter she received these two notes. (*Max hands the two black-mail notes to Hubbard who reads them.*)

HUBBARD. (*Glancing at postmarks.*) Last February. (*To Margot.*) How many times have you seen this man?

MARGOT. (*Angrily.*) I've never seen him.

HUBBARD. (*To Max, briskly.*) Mr. Halliday, I'd like you to come along with us.

MAX. Yes, of course.

HUBBARD. Mrs. Wendice, when you come to make your statement there may be other police officers present. I shall warn you first that anything you say will be taken down and may be used in evidence. Now, never mind what you've told me so far. We'll forget all about that. From now on tell us exactly what you know about this man and exactly what happened last night. If you try and conceal anything at all it may put you in a very serious position.

MARGOT. I wish you'd explain what you mean by all this.

HUBBARD. I will You admit that you killed this man. (*Tony enters quietly from garden and stands listening.*) You say you did it in self-defense. Unfortunately, there were no witnesses, so we've only your word for that.

TONY. But I heard it all—over the telephone, Inspector.

HUBBARD. (*Turning to Tony.*) What exactly did you hear, Mr. Wendice?

TONY. I heard—well, I heard a thud and . . .

HUBBARD. Did you hear anything to indicate that a struggle was going on?

TONY. Well, what I heard was perfectly consistent with what my wife told me.

HUBBARD. So all you really know of the matter is what your wife told you, isn't it? (*To Margot.*) You suggest that this man came to burgle your flat, but there's no evidence of that. There is evidence, however, that he was blackmailing you.

TONY. Blackmail?

MAX. It's true, Tony.

HUBBARD. You suggest that he came in by the window—and we know he came in by that door.

MARGOT. (*Frantically.*) But he can't have got in that way. That door was locked and there are only two keys. (*Fumbling in her handbag.*) My husband had his with him and mine was in my handbag. . . . (*Takes out her latchkey and holds it up.*) Here! (*There is a pause.*)

HUBBARD. (*Quietly.*) You could have let him in. (*Pause.*)

TONY. You're not suggesting that she let him in herself?

HUBBARD. At present, that appears to be the only way he could have entered.

MARGOT. Don't you even believe I was attacked? (*Puts her hand to her throat.*) How do you think I got these bruises on my throat?

HUBBARD. You could have caused those bruises yourself. A silk stocking was found outside the window. It had two knots tied in it. Does that mean anything to you?

MARGOT. I suppose that must have been the stocking he used. (*Pause.*)

HUBBARD. We found the twin stocking wrapped in newspaper at the bottom of the wastepaper basket. Can you explain why your attacker should do that?

MARGOT. No.

HUBBARD. Those stockings were yours, weren't they?

MARGOT. (*Horrified.*) No!

HUBBARD. We know they were. One of the heels had been darned with some silk that didn't quite match. We found a reel of that silk in your mending basket. (*Margot rushes to mending basket and searches inside.*)

MARGOT. (*Thoroughly frightened.*) Tony, there was a pair of stockings in here. (*Tony goes to desk. picks up phone and dials frantically.*)

TONY. (*As he dials.*) I've heard of police deliberately planting clues to make sure of a conviction. I just didn't realize they did it in this country.

MARGOT. (*Running across to Tony.*) His men were in here for hours last night. They could easily have taken those stockings out and done anything with them.

TONY. Of course they did. And they wiped his shoes on the door mat as well. (*Margot turns to Max.*)

ROGER. (*Offstage, heard through receiver.*) Hullo.

TONY. (*Into phone.*) Hullo, Roger. Tony Wendice, here. Now listen, Roger—we had a burglary last night. And Margot was attacked.

ROGER. Margot! Was she hurt?

TONY. No, she's all right, but the man was killed. The police are here now. And don't laugh—but they're suggesting that Margot killed him intentionally. . . .

HUBBARD. (*Interrupting.*) I wouldn't say that if I were you.

ROGER. Well! That's a good one!

TONY. It's funny, isn't it? Now, can you come round at once? To the Maida Vale Police Station. . . .

ROGER. Be there right away.

TONY. Thanks, old boy. Good-bye. (*Tony rings off and crosses to*

55

Margot.) It's all right, darling, Roger's going to meet us at the police station.

HUBBARD. Mr. Wendice, I should advise you . . .

TONY. Our lawyer will give us all the advice we need, thank you. (*Tony and Margot start to exit through French window. Max sees handbag on sofa.*)

MAX. Here's your bag, Margot. (*Tony opens French window.*)

MARGOT. Oh, thank you, Max. (*She takes bag, looks around the room, thoroughly bewildered. She turns and exits by French window. Max follows her out. Hubbard is about to exit, then turns to Tony.*)

HUBBARD. You are coming, sir?

TONY. But of course, Inspector.

HUBBARD. (*Mumbling, half to himself.*) Mm—I see—yes—I just wondered . . . (*Hubbard exits. Tony gives a brief glance around the room. He is now in complete control of the situation. He puts his hands in his pockets and follows Hubbard out. He closes and locks French windows behind him.*)

CURTAIN

ACT III

SCENE 1

The same. A few months later. Early afternoon.

The furniture has been rearranged. Curtains open but shutters have been fastened. No light except sharp rays through shutters. On the desk are a bottle of whiskey and a glass. The wastepaper basket is overflowing with odd junk and crumpled newspapers. Next to this there is a paper carrier containing groceries. The oblong table that was behind the sofa in preceding scenes is now U. L. under bookcase. A small radio is on this table. A bed has been brought into the room L. C. It has not been made properly for several days. Against the fireplace is the sofa. Odd clothing and robe are thrown over the sofa. On the floor is Tony's leather suitcase with the lid open, half packed. An electric heater stands on floor between sofa and bed, and is plugged in. A metal ice pick with bottles and glasses are on bottom shelf of R. bookcase.

When the curtain rises the room is in darkness. (NOTE: During this act Tony, Margot and Hubbard should wear special shoes so that their footsteps can be well heard in the passage, when necessary.) Footsteps are heard in the passage outside and a key turns in the hall door. Tony enters. He wears a raincoat, and carries a small blue fiber attaché case. Tony switches on the lights. He takes key out of door and puts it in raincoat pocket, then takes raincoat off. He puts raincoat on chair in hall. Closes door. He puts attaché case on bed, looks at watch, then crosses to table. He turns on radio. He returns to attaché case and unlocks it. He takes out a wad of pound notes, about 50, puts it in pocket and relocks case. Radio fades in. He looks up at the set and listens intently.

ANNOUNCER. . . . The main obstacles were the export of fruit and vegetables. Agreement has now been reached that the export

58

quotas originally asked for be lowered by twelve and a half per cent. (*Pause.*) The Home Secretary has written to the lawyers of Mrs. Margot Wendice to say that he has decided that there are not sufficient grounds to justify his recommending a reprieve. At the Old Bailey last November Mrs. Wendice was found guilty of the murder of Charles Alexander Swann and was sentenced to death. (*Pause.*) The official forecast is that there will be bright periods and showers in all districts today. Frost is expected again tonight, especially in the South. (*Phone rings.*) The time is now eleven minutes past one and that is the end of the news . . . (*Tony switches off radio and crosses to phone on desk.*)

TONY. (*Into phone.*) Hullo!

PENDLETON. (*Offstage, heard through receiver.*) Mr. Wendice?

TONY. Yes?

PENDLETON. Pendleton here.

TONY. Oh, good afternoon.

PENDLETON. Have you decided about the letters?

TONY. Yes—I'll be quite frank with you—the cost of the defense has been very high. I shall have to ask for five hundred pounds.

PENDLETON. Five hundred! But I'm only asking for her letters . . .

TONY. That's all very well—how would you like your wife's letters read by millions of people?

PENDLETON. I'm prepared to offer three fifty . . .

TONY. No, I'm sorry. I've quite made up my mind.

PENDLETON. Could you give me a little time to think this over?

TONY. By all means, think it over—only I'm going away the day after tomorrow. (*The door buzzer. Tony glances anxiously at the door. Quietly.*) Excuse me. I shall have to ring you back. (*He rings off. Goes to hall door and opens it. Max stands in the passage outside. He wears neither coat nor hat. They stare at each other for a moment or two.*)

MAX. Hullo, Tony.

TONY. Hullo, Max.

MAX. May I come in?

TONY. Of course, you're quite a stranger.

MAX. (*Entering.*) I'm sorry I haven't been around before. I wasn't sure how you felt—after . . .

TONY. That's all right. It's rather chilly in here. I'll switch on . . . (*Tony stops short as he sees attaché case on bed.*) I'll switch

59

on the fire. Let's find somewhere for you to sit. (*Tony picks up his robe from sofa and throws it over attaché case to hide it from Max.*) I've hardly seen anyone for weeks. I'm getting quite used to it. I've had to move in here because everybody stops in the street and peers in at the bedroom window. When the appeal failed they started climbing into the garden. You can't blame them, I suppose—it's cheaper than the zoo and far more topical.

MAX. I—had to come—in case there was anything . . . (*Tony takes a typed letter from his pocket and hands it to Max.*)

TONY. (*Quietly.*) I'm afraid it's settled, Max. Our lawyer received this from the Home Secretary this morning. (*Max reads letter and hands it back to Tony.*)

MAX. You mustn't give up trying. It's not over yet.

TONY. I'm afraid it is. (*Sits on bed.*) We've done all we can. I went to the prison this morning to—say good-bye, but she wouldn't see me. I was rather glad—she never did like good-byes. (*Pause. Simply.*) I shan't see her again.

MAX. Tony. I take it you'd do anything—to save her life?

TONY. (*Surprised.*) Of course.

MAX. Even if it meant going to prison for several years?

TONY. (*After a pause.*) I'd do absolutely anything.

MAX. I think you can—I'm certain. (*Slowly.*) If you tell the police *exactly* the right story.

TONY. The right story?

MAX. Listen, Tony. I've been working this out for weeks. Just in case it came to this. It may be her only chance.

TONY. Let's have it.

MAX. You'll have to tell the police that you hired Swann to murder her. (*Long pause. Tony can only stare at Max.*)

TONY. (*Rises.*) What are you talking about?

MAX. It's all right, Tony—I've been writing this stuff for years. I know what I'm doing. Margot was convicted because no one would believe her story. Prosecution made out that she was telling one lie after another—and the jury believed him. But what did his case amount to? Only three things. My letter—her stocking, and the idea that, because no key was found on Swann, she must have let him in herself. (*Pause.*) Now Swann is dead. You can tell any story you like about him. You can say that you did know him. That you'd met him, and worked out the whole thing together. Now the blackmail. Swann was only suspected of blackmail for

60

two reasons. Because my letter was found in his pocket and because you saw him the day Margot's bag was stolen.

TONY. Well?

MAX. You can now tell the police that you never saw him at Victoria. That the whole thing was an invention of yours to try and
connect him with the letter.

TONY. But the letter was found in his pocket.

MAX. Because you put it there.

TONY. (Pause.) You mean I should pretend that I stole her handbag?

MAX. Sure. You could have.

TONY. But why?

MAX. Because you wanted to find out who was writing to her.
When you read my letter you were so mad you decided to teach
her a lesson.

TONY. But I can't say that I wrote those blackmail notes.

MAX. Why not? No one can prove that you didn't. (Tony thinks
it over.)

TONY. All right. I stole her bag and blackmailed her. What else?

MAX. You kept my letter and planted it on Swann after he'd been
killed.

TONY. Wait a minute—when could I have done that?

MAX. After you got back from the party and before the police
arrived. At the same time you took one of Margot's stockings from
the mending basket and substituted it for whatever Swann had
used. (Tony thinks it over.)

TONY. Max, I know you're trying to help but—can you imagine
anyone believing this?

MAX. You've got to make them believe it.

TONY. But I wouldn't know what to say. You'd have to come
with me.

MAX. No. I couldn't do that. They know the sort of stuff I write.
If they suspected we'd talked this out they wouldn't even listen.
They mustn't know I've been here.

TONY. Max! It's ridiculous. Why should I want anyone to murder Margot?

MAX. Oh, one of the stock motives. Had Margot made a will?
(Pause.)

TONY. I—yes, I believe she had.

MAX. Are you the main beneficiary?

TONY. I suppose so.

MAX. Well, there you are.

TONY. But thousands of husbands and wives leave money to each other, without murdering each other. The police wouldn't believe a word of it! They'd take it for exactly what it is. A husband desperately trying to save his wife.

MAX. Well, it's worth a try. They can't hang you for planning a murder that never came off. Face it. The most you'd get would be a few years in prison.

TONY. Thanks very much.

MAX. . . . And you'd have saved her life. That doesn't seem too big a price.

TONY. That's fine coming from you, Max. Her life might not be in danger at all if it hadn't been for you. It was because of your—association with her that she lost the sympathy of the jury. Don't get me wrong, Max. If there was the slightest chance of this coming off—of course I'd do it. But it's got to be convincing. How—how could I have persuaded Swann to do a thing like this?

MAX. You'd have to say you offered him money.

TONY. What money? I haven't got any. (*Pause.*)

MAX. You would have Margot's money.

TONY. It would be months before I could lay my hands on that. And people don't commit murder on credit. No, we'll have to think up something better than that . . .

MAX. All right—we will. There is an answer and we've got to find it. (*Pause.*) How much time have we got?

TONY. (*As though he can hardly say the words.*) It's tomorrow morning . . . (*Offstage door slams. Footsteps. Door buzzer.*)

MAX. Sssssssh! (*They stop and listen. They look at each other. Tony goes to open the hall door. Max snaps his fingers to attract Tony's attention. He motions Tony to wait and crosses quietly and exits into kitchen. When Tony opens the hall door Inspector Hubbard is standing in the passage outside. He carries a raincoat over his arm and a brief case.*)

TONY. Oh—hullo, Inspector. (*Hubbard enters and Tony closes the door. Anxiously.*) Is it—about my wife?

HUBBARD. (*Sympathetically.*) Er—no, sir. I'm afraid not.

TONY. (*Surprised.*) What is it, then? (*While they talk Hubbard hangs his brief case on the same chair as Tony's raincoat and then hangs up his hat and raincoat on coat rack.*)

HUBBARD. (*Hanging things up.*) I'm making inquiries in connection with a robbery that took place about three weeks ago.

TONY. Can't this wait a few days?

HUBBARD. (*Sincerely.*) Of course, sir, I'm very conscious of your position. If I may—I would like to say how deeply sorry I am that things . . .

TONY. (*Curtly.*) Yes, Inspector—all right. How can I help you?

HUBBARD. The cashier of a factory in Ledbury Street was attacked in his office and two men made off with several hundred pounds—mostly in pound notes.

TONY. What's all this got to do with me?

HUBBARD. In cases like this, all police divisions are asked to keep a lookout for anyone spending large sums of money. (*He pauses as if expecting Tony to say something.*)

TONY. I see.

HUBBARD. I was wondering if you had sold anything recently—for cash.

TONY. Why?

HUBBARD. My sergeant happened to be making inquiries at Wales' garage the other day. (*Pause.*) It appears that you settled an account there recently for—(*Glancing at notebook.*)—just over sixty pounds.

TONY. (*Casually.*) Yes. I happened to have quite a lot on me at the time so I paid cash.

HUBBARD. I see. Had you just drawn this money from your bank? (*Pause.*)

TONY. (*On his guard.*) Have you been to my bank, Inspector?

HUBBARD. (*With a smile.*) As a matter of fact, I have. They wouldn't help me. Bank statements are always jealously guarded. (*Good-naturedly.*) Where'd you get it, sir?

TONY. Is that any of your business?

HUBBARD. If it was stolen money—yes, sir. It is my business. (*Taking out his pipe and holding it up.*) Do you mind if I smoke?

TONY. Go ahead. (*With a laugh.*) Do you really think I've been receiving stolen money?

HUBBARD. Until you tell where you got it—I shan't know what to think—shall I? (*Hubbard feels around in his pockets and then goes to hall and takes a tobacco pouch from one of the pockets of his raincoat.*) You see, if you got that money from someone you didn't know—well, that might be the very person we're looking

63

for. Hullo! (*He stoops down and appears to pick up something from the carpet just beneath his raincoat.*) Is this yours, sir? (*He holds up a latchkey.*)

TONY. (*Moving nearer.*) What is it?

HUBBARD. (*Casually.*) Somebody's latchkey. It was lying on the floor—just here. (*Tony crosses to hall and feels in the pockets of his raincoat. From one of them he takes out his latchkey and holds it up.*)

TONY. No. I've got mine here. (*At the same time Hubbard opens hall door and tries to fit the other key into the lock.*)

HUBBARD. No. It's not yours. (*Tony puts his key back into his raincoat pocket.*) It may be mine, then. (*Feeling in pockets of his raincoat.*) Yes, it is. It must have dropped out of my pocket. There's a small hole here. (*He walks a few paces back into the room, looking at key in his hand. Continuing as he goes.*) That's the trouble with those keys—they're all alike. (*He puts key carefully into his side pocket.* NOTE: *This is important so as to emphasize that Hubbard's key is not still in Hubbard's raincoat.*) I'm sorry, sir, you were saying . . .?

TONY. I—I don't think I was . . .

HUBBARD. Oh, yes—about that money—I'd be grateful if you'd tell me where you got it. After all, a hundred pounds is quite a lot to carry around.

TONY. You said sixty a moment ago.

HUBBARD. Did I? Oh—yes—my sergeant decided to dig a little deeper before he put in his report. (*Pulling at his pipe.*) He said you'd also paid—a bill at your tailor's and another—for wines and spirits.

TONY. I'm sorry he went to all that trouble. If he'd come straight to me, I could have explained it at once. I simply won rather a large sum at dog racing.

HUBBARD. Over a hundred pounds? (*Tony glances anxiously toward the kitchen door.*)

TONY. (*Quietly.*) Yes, over a hundred pounds. It has been done before, you know.

HUBBARD. I see. (*Smiling.*) Why didn't you tell me this straight away, sir?

TONY. (*Coldly.*) Because I'm a little ashamed to be caught going to dog racing when my wife is under sentence of death.

HUBBARD. (*Sympathetically.*) I know how it is sir. Helps to take your mind off things. (*Moving to hall.*) Well, that answers everything, doesn't it? I'm sorry to have had to bother you at this time.

TONY. (*Going to open hall door.*) Not at all. (*Hubbard takes his hat off the peg and then turns to Tony just as Tony is about to open door.*)

HUBBARD. (*Casually.*) Oh, there is just one other thing, sir. Have you a small blue attaché case? (*Tony is obviously shaken by this. He does not reply for several seconds.*)

TONY. Don't say you've found it already? (*Hubbard strolls back into the room.*)

HUBBARD. Why? Have you lost it?

TONY. Yes. I was going to report it this afternoon. I think I left it in a taxi. How did you know about that attaché case, Inspector? (*Hubbard watches Tony closely, takes out pad and pencil from his pocket. The door of the kitchen opens a little, but neither Tony nor Hubbard notices it.*)

HUBBARD. The wine shop mentioned that you had it when you paid your bill. So my sergeant checked back on your garage and your tailor. They both remembered you having it with you when you paid them.

TONY. Yes. I use it instead of a brief case.

HUBBARD. (*Going to hall door.*) Well, these taxi-men are pretty good at turning things in. I hope you'll find it all right. (*Enter Max from kitchcen.*) Oh! Mr. Halliday. (*Max stands there staring curiously at Tony.*)

MAX. Before you go, Inspector—I think Mr. Wendice has something to tell you.

HUBBARD. Oh, has he? (*Hubbard turns to Tony. Tony stares at Max. Max goes to sofa and looks under some of Tony's clothes.*)

MAX. Where did you put it, Tony?

TONY. (*At bed.*) What's come over you?

MAX. (*Crossing to bed.*) When I was in here just now there was a small attaché case. I can't remember just where I saw it but . . . (*Max lifts Tony's dressing gown and reveals the case. He carries it to desk and tries to open it but it is locked.*) Got the key, Tony?

TONY. Have you gone mad? (*Max takes metal ice pick from drinks tray on bottom shelf of R. bookcase.*)

MAX. Very well. If there's no key we'll have to open it some other way.

65

HUBBARD. (*To Max.*) Just a moment, sir. (*To Tony, sharply.*) Why did you say you left this in a taxi?

TONY. I thought I had. (*Max is busily working on the lock.*) Don't be a fool, Max. I've got the key somewhere. (*Searching in pockets.*) I don't know what all the fuss is about. . . . (*Max suddenly fixes point of ice pick behind the lock and gives a twist.*) Max, you . . .

MAX. It's all right, Tony, I'll buy you a new one. (*Max opens case and takes out an evening paper and six bundles of one-pound notes. He lays them on the desk. Max stacks them on the desk, one by one. Hubbard throws hat onto bed, crosses to desk and examines the money.*)

HUBBARD. Must be over five hundred pounds here. (*Turning to Tony.*) Where did you get it?

MAX. I can tell you why he got it. That money was to have been paid to a man named Swann—after he had murdered Mrs. Wendice in this room. As you know, there was—an accident—so it wasn't necessary to pay Swann, after all. Obviously he couldn't produce all this without questions being asked—so he lived on it. He's been living on it ever since the twenty-eighth of September.

HUBBARD. (*To Tony.*) Well, Mr. Wendice?

MAX. Just now you said you'd do anything to save Margot. What's made you change your mind?

TONY. (*To Hubbard.*) Before you came, Inspector, he was trying to persuade me to go to the police and tell the most fantastic story you ever heard. Apparently I bribed Swann to murder my wife so that—correct me if I go wrong, Max—so that I could inherit all her money. And that isn't all. You remember that letter of Mr. Halliday's? Well, it wasn't Swann who stole it. I did! And I wrote those two blackmail notes. And I kept Mr. Halliday's letter and planted it on the body. . . .

MAX. (*To Hubbard.*) And that stocking which was found . . .

TONY. Oh, yes—the stocking. Perhaps I'd better tell this. It may sound more like a confession. I substituted . . . (*To Max.*) Is that the right word? I substituted one of my wife's stockings for—er—the other one—you follow me, don't you? Er—what else, Max?
(*Max goes to hall door and opens it.*)

MAX. (*To Hubbard.*) He told Swann he would hide his key somewhere out here. (*He looks up and feels along the ledge above and outside the door.*) Probably on this ledge. Swann let himself in,

66

then hid behind the curtains. Then Wendice phoned from the hotel and brought her . . . (*Tony sits on bed.*)

HUBBARD. Just a minute. If Swann had used Mr. Wendice's key —it would still have been on him when he died. Besides, how did Mr. Wendice get in when he returned from the hotel? (*Pause.*)

MAX. (*Thinking it out as he goes.*) She could have let him in— and he could have taken his key out of Swann's pocket before the police arrived.

HUBBARD. But he let himself in with his own key. That was established at the trial—don't you remember? (*Max appears defeated by this.*)

TONY. Come on, Max—your move. (*Max goes to hall door and looks up again at the ledge outside. As he speaks he demonstrates.*)

MAX. (*Slowly, but not overemphasized.*) Swann could have taken the key from here—unlocked the door—and then returned it to the ledge before he went in.

HUBBARD. (*Interrupting.*) All right, Mr. Halliday. This is all very interesting, but it isn't getting me any nearer what I came to find out.

MAX (*Frantic.*) But this is a matter of life and death. What else matters?

HUBBARD. What matters to me is where Mr. Wendice got this money, that's all I want to know. (*Max closes the door and crosses quickly to desk.*)

MAX. We'll soon find out how long he's had it. (*Max starts to go through top drawer.*)

TONY. Now, what's the matter? (*Max takes out a checkbook and examines the stubs.*)

MAX. (*Excitedly showing checkbook to Hubbard.*) There you are, Inspector. The last check he wrote was on the twenty-seventh of September. That was the day before this happened. I tell you he's been living off it ever since. (*Hubbard looks through the checkbook stubs.*) Here's his bank statement. (*Max opens drawer and takes out the black folder. He opens it on the desk and examines the entries.*)

HUBBARD. (*Looking at bank statement.*) He hasn't drawn any large sums from his bank. Nothing over—fifty-three pounds. (*Hubbard drops folder on desk. Max picks it up and examines it.*)

MAX. But just look at these, Inspector—nearly every week—

thirty-five pounds—forty—thirty-five—forty-five . . . He could have saved it up.

TONY. Of course—I may have been planning all this for years!

MAX. (*Threatening.*) Where did you get it?

TONY. Are you sure you want to know? (*To Max, grimly.*) I warn you, Max, you won't like it.

MAX. Come on.

TONY. (*Rises.*) Very well—you asked for it. (*Pause.*) When she called me back from the party that night I found her kneeling beside Swann and going through his pockets. She kept saying he had something of hers—but she couldn't find it. She was almost hysterical. That's why I wouldn't let the police question her. In the state she was in she would have told every lie under the sun. The next morning she showed me that money—just like it is now—all in one-pound notes. She said, "If anything happens to me—don't let them find this." (*Pause.*) After she was arrested I took the money in that case to Charing Cross Station and left it in the checkroom. Whenever I needed money I took it out and left it in some other checkroom. I knew that if you found it she wouldn't stand a chance. You see, she was just about to give it to him when she killed him instead.

MAX. Do you expect anyone to believe this?

TONY. I've really no idea. What about it, Inspector? (*Pause.*)

HUBBARD. Hmmmmmmmm? (*At desk.*) Well, it certainly seems to fit in with the verdict at the trial.

MAX. (*Frantic.*) You mean you're not even going to check up on this? She's being hanged tomorrow. (*Tony goes to bed.*)

HUBBARD. (*Wearily.*) All this has been out of my hands for months. There's been a trial and an appeal . . .

MAX. Of course, it wouldn't do you much good, would it? You'd have to admit you arrested the wrong person.

TONY. (*To Max.*) I think you ought to go.

MAX. You bet I'll go. (*Goes to hall.*) But you've made one mistake. (*Pause.*) What will happen when Margot hears about all this? (*Pause.*)

TONY. She'll deny it, of course.

MAX. And perhaps she'll change her will. (*This gets under Tony's skin. Max opens hall door. He looks straight at Tony. Slowly.*) You'll have done it all for nothing. (*Max exits. From now on Hub-*

68

bard speaks to Tony very gently, almost as if he was a child. Tony turns to Hubbard.)
TONY. Suppose I had told that story of his. Would anyone have believed me?
HUBBARD. Not a chance, sir. Before nearly every execution someone comes forward like this. This must have been very distressing for you—coming as it did. *(Tony sits on bed.)*
TONY. Do you think they'll let him see her? I—I don't want her upset just . . .
HUBBARD. Have a word with your lawyer. He might be able to prevent it. *(Nodding at money on desk.)* And I should get all that money into the bank before someone pinches it.
TONY. Thank you—I think I will.
HUBBARD. *(Taking down hat from peg.)* By the way, I was asked to tell you—there are a few things belonging to Mrs. Wendice at the police station.
TONY. What sort of things?
HUBBARD. Just some books—and a handbag, I believe. They'd like you to come and collect them sometime.
TONY. You mean—after tomorrow?
HUBBARD. Yes—or today, if you like. Just ask the desk sergeant —he knows all about it. *(Hubbard takes his own hat and raincoat from coat rack left of door, then changes it for Tony's raincoat on chair in hall, leaving his own raincoat in place of Tony's, picks up briefcase, crosses to Tony and puts out his hand. NOTE: This must be done very smoothly as Hubbard is talking. Tony must be looking the other way and does not notice all this.)* Well, good-bye, Mr. Wendice. I don't suppose we shall meet again.
TONY. *(Shaking hands.)* Good-bye, Inspector—and thank you. *(Hubbard exits at hall door. Tony waits till he hears the street door slam. Then he crosses to desk and pours whiskey into a glass and drinks it. He picks up one of the bundles of notes and whisks it like a pack of cards. He picks up attaché case, examines lock, throws it on bed and looks around the room. He picks up the paper carrier bag, tips contents on desk, fills bag with bundles of notes, covers them with newspaper. He crosses to bed, leans across it and switches off electric heater. He then crosses to hall with paper bag and takes Hubbard's raincoat and throws it over his arm. He switches off light and exits at hall door. Sound of footsteps and street door opening and slamming. The pink glow of electric heater*

69

dies slowly. There is a sound of key in lock. The hall door opens and Hubbard enters. He switches on small flashlight and looks around the room. He looks at key and then pockets it carefully. He throws his briefcase and raincoat on the bed and crosses to the desk. He picks up the phone and dials a number.)

POLICE. *(Offstage, heard through receiver.)* Maida Vale Police.

HUBBARD. Chief Inspector here. Give me Sergeant O'Brien quick. *(Pause.)*

O'BRIEN. O'Brien.

HUBBARD. Hubbard . . . Look, I've got back in again. Start the ball rolling.

O'BRIEN. Yes, sir. *(Hubbard rings off. He looks around the desk until he finds Tony's bank statement and starts to examine it again. There is a crash of broken glass from behind shutters. Hubbard puts out flashlight and moves silently into the kitchen. Someone opens the French windows but the shutters bar his way. A knife is inserted through the crack where the shutters meet and the bar which holds them together is lifted off its pin. Shutters fly open, letting daylight into the room. Max enters. He immediately goes to desk and starts searching for something. Hubbard appears from kitchen.)*

HUBBARD. What are you up to? *(Max looks up, startled.)* What's the idea?

MAX. Where's his bank statement?

HUBBARD. Never mind about that. You've got to get out of here—quick.

MAX. *(Raising his voice.)* Have you got it?

HUBBARD. Sssssh! Not so loud.

MAX. But don't you see . . .

HUBBARD. *(Savagely, but in half-whisper.)* Shut up! *(Almost frantic.)* If you want to save Mrs. Wendice, keep quiet and let me handle this.

MAX. You? *(Sound of street door opening, footsteps. Hubbard raises his hand to keep Max quiet and then points to hall door.)*

HUBBARD. Sssssssh! *(They both stand motionless watching the hall door. Sound of someone trying to insert key into lock. Then silence for a moment. Door buzzer. Pause. Buzzer again. Hubbard raises his hand to restrain any movement from Max. Footsteps move away. Sound of street door shutting. Hubbard breathes a sigh of relief. He opens bedroom door and peers toward the street.)* Whew!

70

You nearly ditched us then. I should have locked you up.

MAX. What is all this?

HUBBARD. (*Letting off steam.*) They talk about flatfooted policemen! May the saints protect us from the gifted amateur! (*He crosses to the open window and looks out into the garden for several seconds. Quietly.*) You'd better prepare yourself for a surprise, Mr. Halliday. (*Hubbard continues to stare outside and then suddenly backs into the room waving Max away from the window. After several seconds Margot appears from window, followed by Thompson, a police constable in uniform. Margot is dressed in the same clothes as she was wearing at the end of Act Two, and she carries the same handbag. She stops in the window as she sees the two men. Her appearance should indicate that she has been through a great deal during the last two or three monthbs.*)

MARGOT. Hello, Max. (*Max goes to her.*) Where's Tony?

MAX. He—he's gone out.

MARGOT. When will he be back?

HUBBARD. (*His manner is official and brisk.*) We're not sure. All right, Thompson. (*Thompson exits through window, Hubbard turns to Margot.*) Was it you who rang just now?

MARGOT. Yes. (*Surprised.*) Why didn't you let me in?

HUBBARD. You've got a key. Why didn't you use it?

MARGOT. I did. But it didn't fit the lock.

HUBBARD. And you know why—don't you?

MARGOT. No, I don't. (*Pause.*) Has the lock been changed?

HUBBARD. May I have your bag? (*Margot gives him her handbag. Hubbard opens it, undoes the zip purse and takes out the key. He holds it up.*) You knew this wasn't your key, didn't you?

MARGOT. No. (*Hubbard picks up the attaché case from the bed. He shows it to her.*)

HUBBARD. Your husband has explained this, you know. You can tell us all about it now. (*Margot stares at it. Hubbard watches her face.*)

MARGOT. (*Bewildered.*) What is it? Why am I . . . ? I don't understand. (*Hubbard looks at her steadily for a moment.*)

HUBBARD. No. I don't believe you do. (*Kindly.*) Come and sit down, Mrs. Wendice. (*Margot crosses to sofa and sits down. Hubbard puts key and purse back into handbag.*)

MAX. What's going on here? (*Hubbard goes to desk and looks out of window.*)

HUBBARD (*Shouting into garden.*) Thompson!

THOMPSON. (*From garden.*) Sir. (*Thompson enters.*)

HUBBARD. Take this handbag to the police station.

THOMPSON. Yes, sir. (*Thompson slips his arm through the straps of the handbag and exits through French window.*)

HUBBARD. Wait a minute, you clot. You can't go down the street like that. (*Hubbard takes his briefcase from desk and exits into garden.*) Put it in this.

MAX. Margot, what is this? Why are you here?

MARGOT. (*As if in a dream.*) I don't know. (*Slowly.*) About an hour ago the warden came to see me. He just said I was to be taken home. Two detectives drove me here. They parked just around the corner. Then that policeman came up and said I could go. But I couldn't get this door open. When I left the policeman was still outside and he brought me around by the garden. (*Getting up.*) Where's Tony? He was supposed to visit me this morning but they said he couldn't come. Has anything happened to him?

MAX. No—nothing. (*Hubbard enters through French window from garden. He closes the window, locks it and closes shutters. Then he goes to hall and switches on light.*) Inspector, do you think you could tell us what you're up to?

HUBBARD. Mrs. Wendice, what I've got to tell you may come as a shock.

MARGOT. Yes?

HUBBARD. We strongly suspect that your husband had planned to murder you. (*Margot stares at Hubbard for a moment and then turns to Max.*)

MAX. He's right, Margot. He arranged for Swann to come here that night and kill you. (*Margot shows no sign of emotion.*)

MARGOT. How long have you known this?

HUBBARD. (*Surprised.*) Did you suspect it yourself?

MARGOT. (*Working it out in her mind.*) No—never—and yet . . . (*She looks around the room then turns suddenly to Max.*) What's the matter with me, Max? I don't seem able to feel anything. Shouldn't I break down or something?

MAX. It's delayed action, that's all. In a couple of days you're going to have one hellava breakdown. (*Puts an arm around her. To Hubbard.*) When did you find out?

HUBBARD. The first clue came quite by accident. We discovered that your husband had been spending large numbers of pound notes all over the place. It ran into over three hundred pounds and it appeared to have started about the time you were arrested. Now, I had to find out where he got this money and how. Then I remembered that after you were arrested, we searched this flat and I saw a copy of his bank statement in that desk. So yesterday afternoon, I went to the prison and asked to see your handbag, and while I was doing this I managed to lift your latchkey. Highly irregular, of course, but my blood was up. Then, this morning when your husband was out, I came here to look at his bank statement. (*Pause.*) I never saw it because I never got through that door. . . . You see, the key I had taken from your handbag didn't fit the lock. (*Three loud knocks on the ceiling above. They all look up and Hubbard rushes to the hall and switches off lights.*) Don't make a sound. (*Sound of a street door opening and shutting. Footsteps move along passage to hall door and stop. Long pause and then footsteps move away.* NOTE: *Tony does not put key in door this time. He hasn't got one. Street door opens and slams. After a few moments Hubbard goes and opens the hall door. Calling up.*) Williams.

WILLIAMS. (*From upstairs.*) Sir.

HUBBARD. Who was it?

WILLIAMS. Wendice, sir.

HUBBARD. Which way did he go?

WILLIAMS. Hold on. (*Pause.*) Towards the police station, sir.

HUBBARD. Good. (*Hubbard closes hall door and switches on lights. Crosses to telephone.*) That was a near one. (*Picks up phone and dials a number.*) Maida Vale Police?

O'BRIEN. (*Off stage, on phone.*) Yes, sir. O'Brien.

HUBBARD. Hubbard here . . . Look, O'Brien, he's found out about his raincoat. . . . He just came back and couldn't get in. I think he's on his way to the station now. Has Thompson arrived with the handbag?

O'BRIEN. Yes, sir.

HUBBARD. Good. Now, look—give Wendice those books and the handbag and make sure he sees the key. . . . Better make him check the contents and sign for it. If he wants his own key and raincoat . . . er, tell him I've gone to Glasgow.

O'BRIEN. Yes, sir.

HUBBARD. Any questions?

O'BRIEN. No questions.

HUBBARD. Right . . . Call me back when he leaves the station.
. . . (*During the phone call Max moves slowly to hall door and opens it. He looks up thoughtfully at the ledge above the door, then stares down at the spot where Swann died and then back to the ledge. He feels along it with his fingers and looks puzzled. To Max, as he rings off.*) Well, Mr. Halliday, have you got it?
MAX. (*Puzzled.*) I don't think so. (*Slowly.*) Where is Mrs. Wendice's key? (*Hubbard goes through open hall door into passage. He takes her key from under the stair carpet and holds it up. Then he replaces it exactly in the same place.*)
HUBBARD. It took me just half an hour to find it.
MAX. But if it was there—why didn't Wendice use it just now?
HUBBARD. He didn't use it because he doesn't realize it's there. He still thinks it's in his wife's handbag. You see, you were very nearly right. (*To Margot.*) He told Swann that he would leave your key under the stair carpet, Mrs. Wendice, and told him to return it to the same place when he left. But as Swann was killed he naturally assumed that your key would still be in one of Swann's pockets. That was his little mistake. Because Swann had done exactly what you suggested, Mr. Halliday. (*Going through the motions.*) He unlocked the door—and then returned the key *before* he came in. . . .
MAX. And it's been out there ever since! And the key Wendice took out of Swann's pocket and returned to her handbag was . . .
HUBBARD. Swann's own latchkey! Mind you, even I didn't guess that at once. At first I thought your husband must have changed the lock. It had always surprised me that no key was found on Swann's body. After all, most men carry a latchkey about with them. Then I had a brainwave. I took the key that was in your handbag to Mrs. Van Dorn's and unlocked the door of her apartment. Then I borrowed her telephone and called Scotland Yard.
MARGOT. Why did you bring me back here?
HUBBARD. Because you were the only other person who could possibly have left that key outside. I had to find out if you knew it was there.
MARGOT. Suppose I had known?
HUBBARD. (*With a smile.*) Er . . . You didn't!
MARGOT. (*Suddenly.*) Max!
MAX. Yes, darling?
MARGOT. I think I'm going to have that breakdown right now
74

(*Margot turns her head into Max's shoulder and begins to cry softly. Max puts his arms around her. Phone rings.*)

HUBBARD. O'Brien?

O'BRIEN. Yes, sir. He's just left the station.

HUBBARD. Right! (*Rings off. To Margot and Max as he crosses to hall door.*) Try and hang on a little longer! (*Opens door and calls upstairs.*) Williams!

WILLIAMS. (*Upstairs.*) Sir!

HUBBARD. He's just left the station. . . . Give me a thump if he comes this way.

WILLIAMS. (*From upstairs.*) Right, sir. (*Hubbard closes door and makes sure it is locked properly.*)

MARGOT. (*To Max.*) Handkerchief. (*Max produces his handkerchief and Margot wipes her eyes and gives her nose a good blow.*)

MAX. (*To Hubbard.*) What happens now?

HUBBARD. Sooner or later he'll come back here. As I've pinched his key, he'll have to try the one in the handbag. When that doesn't fit he'll realize his mistake, put two and two together and look under the stair carpet.

MAX. But . . . if he doesn't do that—all this is pure guess work. We can't prove a thing.

HUBBARD. That's perfectly true. (*Slowly, with emphasis, pointing to hall door.*) But once he opens that door—we shall know everything. (*Pause.*)

MAX. What will you do then?

HUBBARD. I'm to phone Scotland Yard. They're standing by for my call now.

MAX. And Mrs. Wendice?

HUBBARD. Will have nothing else to fear . . . (*There are three thumps on the ceiling. Max and Margot stand up. Hubbard switches off the lights and stands by the telephone on desk facing hall. Long silence.*)

MAX. (*Gently.*) All right, Margot?

MARGOT. (*In a whisper.*) Yes—I'm all right. (*Max puts his arms around Margot.*)

HUBBARD. (*Softly.*) Quiet, now, you two. (*There is another long silence and then the sound of the street door opening and shutting. Footsteps to hall door. Pause. Sound of key in lock. It doesn't fit. Long pause. Footsteps moving back to front door. Slam. Max gives*

a start. *He opens bedroom door and peeps through. In whisper.)*
Careful!

MAX. He's going round by the garden. He'll see the broken glass.

HUBBARD. Ssssh! *(Pause.)*

MAX. *(In a low whisper.)* He's coming back.

HUBBARD. He's remembered. *(Long pause. Max closes bedroom door silently and returns to Margot. Sound of street door opening and footsteps along passage to hall door. Silence for a few seconds. . . . Then sound of key in door. The door opens and Tony enters. He is carrying Hubbard's raincoat, Margot's handbag and some books. He stands silhouetted in the doorway and stares at the key in the door. Then he takes it out thoughtfully and stares back at the fifth step of the staircase, and then looks back at the key in his hand. Then he switches on the light and with his back to the audience closes the door shut, then turns and walks into the room. After several paces he sees Margot and Max, stares at Margot for a long moment and then drops the books and the handbag to the ground. Then he turns and sees Hubbard. Suddenly he throws away his raincoat and rushes to the hall door in a panic. He opens the hall door but a Detective in plain clothes moves in from the L. and blocks his way. Tony turns back into the room and stares at Margot. Margot turns her head away from Tony and toward Max. Hubbard looks Tony up and down for a moment, then moves very slowly to the telephone and dials a number.)*

CURTAIN

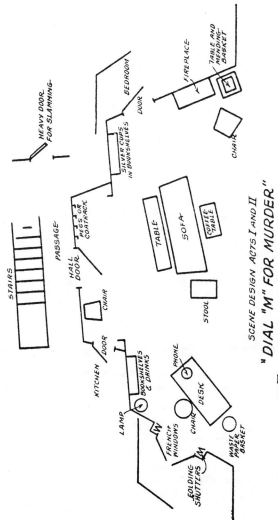

SCENE DESIGN ACTS I AND II

"DIAL "M" FOR MURDER"

ACT III SAME -- BUT BED L.C. AND SOFA AGAINST FIREPLACE

PROPERTY PLOT

Bookcase at R.: liquor bottles and glasses on bottom shelf
Bookcase at L.: silver tennis trophies and tennis racket
Photos on wall around L. bookcase
Clock on mantel
Table behind sofa: silver cigarette case with cigarettes, ash tray, vase of flowers
Small wall table at D. L.: wicker mending basket filled with stockings, scissors, etc.
On desk at R. C.: telephone, address book, desk diary

ACT I
Scene 1

Container of mixed drinks on bottom shelf of R. bookcase
2 glasses with drinks—Max and Margot
Max: matches or lighter, wallet
Margot: 2 white envelopes with letters inside (offstage L.); coat and handbag, also offstage L.
Tony: dinner jacket offstage L.; key, overcoat, handkerchief

Scene 2

White cotton gloves on stool
Brandy bottle and glasses on bottom shelf of bookcase R.
Bundle of pound notes in drawer of desk
Bank statement in drawer of desk
Tony: old leather suitcase (offstage L.); wallet with letter in it
Lesgate: overcoat, pipe and matches in pocket of suit, wrist watch

ACT II
Scene 1

In desk drawer: empty tube of paste
Max's overcoat on coat rack
Leather suitcase (same as last scene) against L. wall of R. bookcase
Bottles of liquor and glasses on drink shelf
Loose clippings and folded newspapers on coffee table
Tony's raincoat on hall chair; in pocket of coat are gloves with key in them
Margot: album of press clippings; off L. is her handbag and in it a small zipper purse and key; offstage R. a cup
Radio on shelf of bookcase R.

Scene 2

Carafe of water and glasses on drink shelf
Margot's handbag, in it bottle of aspirin, zip purse and key, on table
    behind sofa
Suitcase same place as last scene
Lesgate: raincoat, kid gloves, tan silk scarf with tassel ends; key and
    wallet in pocket
Margot: dressing gown
Tony: blanket offstage L.; handkerchief, wallet with letter in it

Scene 3

Blanket folded over desk
Used breakfast dishes and tray on coffee table
Hubbard: notebook and pencil, two snapshots of different sizes
Margot: coat and handbag with key in it (offstage L.)
Max: wallet with two notes in it

Act III

Bottle of whiskey and glass on desk
Wastepaper basket full of newspapers and junk
Large shopping bag of groceries on floor next to wastebasket
Clothing and Tony's robe thrown over sofa
Tony's leather suitcase, lid open, half-packed, on floor
Electric heater, plugged in, on floor between sofa and bed
Bed brought onstage C., sofa moved to in front of fireplace D. L.
Metal ice pick with bottles and glasses on bottom shelf of R. bookcase
In drawer of desk a checkbook and a black folder with bank statements
    in it
Tennis trophies taken out of L. bookcase, which is now empty except
    for tennis racket
Oblong table moved U. L. under bookcase
Radio on oblong table
Tony: raincoat with key in pocket; small blue fiber attaché case with
    wad of paper money (about 50 bills) and a newspaper in it; typed
    letter in pocket of suit; wrist watch; books
Hubbard: small notebook and pencil, key, briefcase, hat, raincoat with
    pouch of tobacco, pipe and matches in pocket, small flashlight
Max: knife, handkerchief
Margot: coat, handbag with zip purse and key in it

NEW PLAYS

★ **SHEL'S SHORTS by Shel Silverstein.** Lauded poet, songwriter and author of children's books, the incomparable Shel Silverstein's short plays are deeply infused with the same wicked sense of humor that made him famous. "...[a] childlike honesty and twisted sense of humor." –*Boston Herald.* "...terse dialogue and an absurdity laced with a tang of dread give [*Shel's Shorts*] more than a trace of Samuel Beckett's comic existentialism." –*Boston Phoenix.* [flexible casting] ISBN: 0-8222-1897-6

★ **AN ADULT EVENING OF SHEL SILVERSTEIN by Shel Silverstein.** Welcome to the darkly comic world of Shel Silverstein, a world where nothing is as it seems and where the most innocent conversation can turn menacing in an instant. These ten imaginative plays vary widely in content, but the style is unmistakable. "...[*An Adult Evening*] shows off Silverstein's virtuosic gift for wordplay...[and] sends the audience out...with a clear appreciation of human nature as perverse and laughable." –*NY Times.* [flexible casting] ISBN: 0-8222-1873-9

★ **WHERE'S MY MONEY? by John Patrick Shanley.** A caustic and sardonic vivisection of the institution of marriage, laced with the author's inimitable razor-sharp wit. "...Shanley's gift for acid-laced one-liners and emotionally tumescent exchanges is certainly potent..." –*Variety.* "...lively, smart, occasionally scary and rich in reverse wisdom." –*NY Times.* [3M, 3W] ISBN: 0-8222-1865-8

★ **A FEW STOUT INDIVIDUALS by John Guare.** A wonderfully screwy comedy-drama that figures Ulysses S. Grant in the throes of writing his memoirs, surrounded by a cast of fantastical characters, including the Emperor and Empress of Japan, the opera star Adelina Patti and Mark Twain. "Guare's smarts, passion and creativity skyrocket to awesome heights..." –*Star Ledger.* "...precisely the kind of good new play that you might call an everyday miracle...every minute of it is fresh and newly alive..." –*Village Voice.* [10M, 3W] ISBN: 0-8222-1907-7

★ **BREATH, BOOM by Kia Corthron.** A look at fourteen years in the life of Prix, a Bronx native, from her ruthless girl-gang leadership at sixteen through her coming to maturity at thirty. "...vivid world, believable and eye-opening, a place worthy of a dramatic visit, where no one would want to live but many have to." –*NY Times.* "...rich with humor, terse vernacular strength and gritty detail..." –*Variety.* [1M, 9W] ISBN: 0-8222-1849-6

★ **THE LATE HENRY MOSS by Sam Shepard.** Two antagonistic brothers, Ray and Earl, are brought together after their father, Henry Moss, is found dead in his seedy New Mexico home in this classic Shepard tale. "...His singular gift has been for building mysteries out of the ordinary ingredients of American family life..." –*NY Times.* "...rich moments ...Shepard finds gold." –*LA Times.* [7M, 1W] ISBN: 0-8222-1858-5

★ **THE CARPETBAGGER'S CHILDREN by Horton Foote.** One family's history spanning from the Civil War to WWII is recounted by three sisters in evocative, intertwining monologues. "...bittersweet music—[a] rhapsody of ambivalence...in its modest, garrulous way...theatrically daring." –*The New Yorker.* [3W] ISBN: 0-8222-1843-7

★ **THE NINA VARIATIONS by Steven Dietz.** In this funny, fierce and heartbreaking homage to *The Seagull*, Dietz puts Chekhov's star-crossed lovers in a room and doesn't let them out. "A perfect little jewel of a play..." –*Shepherdstown Chronicle.* "...a delightful revelation of a writer at play; and also an odd, haunting, moving theater piece of lingering beauty." –*Eastside Journal (Seattle).* [1M, 1W (flexible casting)] ISBN: 0-8222-1891-7

DRAMATISTS PLAY SERVICE, INC.
440 Park Avenue South, New York, NY 10016 212-683-8960 Fax 212-213-1539
postmaster@dramatists.com www.dramatists.com